THE DOCKERS' TRAGEDY

THE
DOCKERS'
TRAGEDY

COLONEL R. B. ORAM

HUTCHINSON OF LONDON

HUTCHINSON & CO *(Publishers)* LTD
178–202 Great Portland Street, London W1

London Melbourne Sydney
Auckland Bombay Toronto
Johannesburg New York

First published 1970

*This book has been set in Baskerville, printed in Great Britain
on Antique Wove paper by Anchor Press, and
bound by Wm. Brendon, both of Tiptree, Essex*

09 100770 4

To Captain A. G. Course
for the encouragement he has given me

ILLUSTRATIONS

DIAGRAMS

INTRODUCTION

In the following pages I have set out to paint a picture of the London dock worker in his work at the docks, where I have known him for half a century. In describing his fortunes since the early 1800s I have kept the narrative as simple as a complex subject will allow. I have, too, given a brief account of the changing work of the docks since the time of George III.

Working customs vary from port to port; there is not even uniform working within the separate docks in the same port. I have avoided introducing details that would have clogged the account of the events that led up to decasualisation and severance payments. While of value to the social historian they would have detracted from its interest to the general reader. I have kept statistics to a minimum; I have not justified each statement of principle with supporting figures.

In telling this story of the docker, with whom for sixteen years I worked day and night, I have used material from my experience in the port of London as a practical dock officer. I have, where appropriate, drawn on my work since retirement as Technical Secretary to the International Cargo Handling Co-ordination Association and also as Maritime Consultant to the United Nations Technical Aid Bureau. Recent assignments to the ports of Yugoslavia and as Port Operations Adviser to the Government of Nationalist China taught me a lot on how ports can be run.

I am glad to have had the opportunity of sketching, very briefly, the part played by the dockers on the Transportation Branch of the Royal Engineers during the Second War. I was proud to command men of their calibre. The full story of the part these men played in helping to win that war would be a book in itself.

During the writing of this history of the dockers my conclusions were confirmed by a letter to *The Port*, from a dockworker. This is a fortnightly journal which, although officially sponsored, maintains a distinctly independent tone. I quote the opening paragraphs what is a very thoughtful letter :

'The Severance Payments Scheme has been agreed and no doubt we shall soon be made aware of just how many men will be required to leave the industry in this first initial stage. We can also be certain that there will be many more required to leave as the employers progress towards the time when they can fully introduce full mobility and flexibility of labour, palletisation, unitisation and containerisation.

'In fact we can see that all the great changes that are envisaged will present a very serious threat to the future social and economic welfare of all portworkers throughout the country.

'Portworkers everywhere must have very great fears for their future and their fears are reflected in their attitude to change. They can hardly be blamed for their suspicion of any new innovations especially since these are generally accompanied with demands for reduced manning scales. They see no solution in the offering of severance payments which to them only represents a buffer to the inevitable task of seeking other employment outside the industry, with sufficient pay to meet their needs.'

Port operators who read this book will find plenty with which to disagree.

For 160 years the docker—the man who loads and discharges general cargo ships—has fought and starved to find a cure for casual employment. This major evil is as old as the industry itself.

On September 18th, 1967 the casual system, which still persisted in modified form, was finally abolished. All registered dock workers became permanent weekly servants of one port employer. The Port of London Authority, for instance, added a further 2,500 men to their permanent force as well as one hundred lightermen.

During the last two decades the handling of general cargo has been so improved that there has been a progressive decline in the demand for dock workers. In April 1968 at least 2,750 men were in excess of the estimated demand in the port of London.

Of what use will the hard-won permanency be if the job has meanwhile disappeared? In 1889 the Great Strike, a bitter fight for 'The Dockers' tanner', lasted for five weeks. Today, dock workers, of whom some could be grandsons of the stalwarts of 1889, are being paid £2,000 to leave the industry.

That, briefly, is the dockers' problem. How it has come about this book will tell. It will explain the processes on the part of the employers, as well as labour, by which the victory has overnight become a near defeat.

I

As a boy of sixteen, I was appointed to the position of a Fourth Class Clerk, the lowest form of clerical life then extant in the PLA.

The date was August 12th, 1912. I arrived at the General Office at London Docks to begin my forty-four years' work in the port of London, a period that lacked nothing in interest. It was to include two wars, a General Strike, a Depression and a second industrial revolution, but I knew nothing of this as I waited for the Principal Examiner, my new chief, to arrive. When in reply to his enquiry I said that I had passed the London University Matriculation with Honours in English, he jumped out of his chair and demanded, 'Why on earth have you come into this place—get out at once.' The unfavourable impression was not relieved when, in response to his bell, there appeared a little, elderly, sandy-featured man, wearing a dusty cut-away coat. I thought he was a stable hand; he was to be my immediate chief for the next twelve months.

'You come along with me, mister.' He never addressed any of his staff other than as 'mister'. Names meant nothing to him but he kept a close watch on us all. And then came the crowning disillusionment—the General Office at London Docks.

This huge building, erected in 1805, and more than one hundred years later substantially unchanged, held about sixty clerks. There was also an office for the Dock Superintendent and his staff. A wide central passage bisected the general office; at the far end a glass box stood, raised on a dais. In this, lord of all he surveyed, reigned the Principal Clerk. On each side of the central gangway, at right angles, were placed lines of high desks, bearing massive cargo ledgers. A row of wooden grilles allowed the carmen to hand their orders through to the ledger clerk. This was the main office for the dock, here the accounts were kept and the charges made out for all the various parcels of goods discharged in the dock or brought there by lighters. The traffic came mainly from the Mediterranean and the near Continental ports. The Ledger divisions had romantic names—Spice and Ivory, South Quay, Wines, Brandies, or the more prosaic Dues on Ships. Merchants who wished to take delivery of their goods applied, through their carmen, to the appropriate ledger clerk. If there was no lien on the goods,[1] authority was given by stamping the order and the carman applied at the department for delivery.

Traffic at the docks was then entirely horse drawn. As a protection from the thunderous noise of the ironshod wheels on the cobbled dock roads, the General Office was fitted with double windows—an early instance of effective double glazing. The noise and the wind-blown straw and dried manure made this compulsory throughout the docks. The carmen were a class that has long disappeared. Dressed in a garb which often included a broken-down top hat of fustian colour, they built up a resistance to the winter cold, from which their vehicles afforded no protection, by adding further layers of overcoats. 'It's three coats warmer today' accurately described a spell of milder weather. There was waged a good-humoured but never-ending war between certain of the carmen, regular applicants at the docks, and the ledger clerks. From the safe side of the partition a carman, known to be touchy, could be baited until he cracked his whip in fury, whilst the clerk declined the offer to 'Come out 'ere and settle it.' At this point the disapproval of the Principal Clerk, unspoken but unmistakable, would end the incident and heads went down again to the ledgers. No carman was seen without his whip. It corresponded to today's ignition key, the symbol of his control of his vehicle. Often the whip had a silver mount and had been in the carman's possession for years. The only time he was known to part with it was to 'pledge' it for an unexpected charge of a shilling or two on the goods he had come to collect. The clerk held the whip, gave the carman credit and within a

[1] The goods had to be clear of H.M. Customs, the freight paid to the shipping company and the Authority's charges for handling the cargo covered before they were released by the ledger clerk responsible.

2

day or two the pledge was redeemed, to the satisfaction of both parties and the saving of paper.

In the winter the office was 'warmed' by two massive open coal fires, unfortunately built on the same side. It was typical of the superior status of the Surrey Commercial Docks that, in their General Office of similar size, twelve fires, six on each side, engaged the continuous stoking of the office keeper. The messenger boys who occasionally put coal on to our fires had a much easier job. After the fashion of the days when they were constructed ninety per cent of the heat went up the chimney. One National Telephone served the whole office; it was used very occasionally for incoming calls. Private calls by the staff were forbidden. There was also a primitive machine for internal dock use and this had a side wheel and handle which you turned until a bell rang. This was the signal to lift the receiver and to hope that the man at the dock department could hear you.

Alongside the Principal Clerk was a division for the Messenger Staff. In the interval between their rounds when they took orders and papers to the several dock departments, they fetched and carried refreshments for the staff. Their spare times were spent in drinking quantities of Camp coffee from thick mugs and eating slabs of dripping toast or scuffling among themselves until cuffed into a reasonable quiet by the Head Messenger, a veteran gunner of the Boer War.

As the junior clerk in the office it was, I suppose, right that my desk should be at the extreme distance from the nearer of the two fires. When the winter of 1912 arrived I learnt what cold meant. By ten in the morning I was looking for a chance to slip down to the basement where one could get from the cook a large mug of hot coffee and a generous round of dripping toast for a penny. The PLA had taken over from the Dock Companies the excellent system of providing staff meals, plus a very few simple amenities. There were in those days, no suitable restaurants in the dock area, neither was the staff allowed to leave the dock during working hours. This basement housed a kitchen presided over by a large and homely cook. In most cases she was the widow of a dock labourer who had met his death whilst at work. If she could cook, the staff were lucky. Next to the kitchen was a large and bare dining room lit by two naked electric bulbs. A small and closely locked cupboard housed the barrel of beer, the property of the staff beer club. I was far too young to join this but I think that draught beer was then twopence a pint. Immediately outside the kitchen and in full view of the dining tables was a battery of six earth closets. They were the only provision made for the staff. When the need arose one applied to one's senior clerk for the key; the time it was issued—and returned—was entered in a book and you placed your initials alongside the entry. In fairness to our senior clerk I can say that he gave you time enough for a surreptitious cigarette. I don't remember that these primitive arrangements were ever the subject of adverse comment. Main drainage was not general in the docks until many years later.

An added discomfort, amounting at the end of each month to mental torture, was the proximity of my desk to the office of the Dock Cashier. Separated only by a window I could not avoid watching an interminable game played by the cashier, a very senior figure, and his assistant. Scraping along on my £4 1s. 8d. paid on the last day of each month, I goggled at the many trays each slotted to hold a thousand golden sovereigns. Larger trays held Bank of England notes, the lowest denomination being £5. They were not the poorly produced and tawdry notes of today that litter the pay desks of multiple stores, but large crinkly pieces of semi-stiff paper, each beautifully embossed and certainly having no place in a working-class budget.

I had been engaged by the PLA to do what was then an accepted method of working but which is becoming increasingly rare today —to do a simple job of work in a simple way; to prevent goods being taken illegally out of the dock. When each delivery had been completed, and the quantity was small because there was nothing bigger than a pair horse van, the carman was given a pass which he surrendered at the dock gate. When the PLA policeman was satisfied, by a visual check, that the load was as stated, the carman was allowed to leave. No pass was valid unless it had been signed by an authorised officer, a record of whose signature was separately available at each dock gate for confirmation. A typical pass might cover 'Joel's single horse van with sixty bags of onions ex *Estrellano*'; it would be signed by one of the departmental officers. It was unthinkable that a carman would attempt to leave the dock without his pass being correctly signed. My job was to examine each

4

pass—there were many hundreds each day—on the day following their issue, and to check it against the endorsement on the delivery order. The importance of the job had been impressed on me by my predecessor who had left the PLA for a more attractive career in a City bank.

This humdrum life was enlivened by occasional scraps of humour. I learnt early that the docks have their own brand of humour, cockney like and direct to the point. Long before the days of the Public Relations Officer (a tentative start was not made by the Authority to establish relations of any kind with the public until the late 1920s) the occasional visit of a party of boys from a school was handled by a clerk whose interest lay more in the break from his work than in a knowledge of the activities of the dock. One such party of boys had recently been taken round the London Docks. Impressed by the shipping which still contained sailing vessels, the highlight of the afternoon came in a visit to a small museum that had, over the years, been formed by a few historically minded members of the staff. Among the exhibits was a large stone ball which had at some time in the past decorated a column now demolished. The next day brought the inevitable school essay, 'What I saw at the London Docks'. The visit had been sponsored by a Member of the Board who was also a prominent figure in LCC education circles. He thought that the essays, which all contained one feature in common, were worth examination by his fellow Member, Sir Joseph Broodbank. The one event that had made the day for every boy was seeing the stone cannon ball that had knocked out Nelson's eye at Trafalgar. Board Members have never been noted for a sense of humour and Sir Joseph demanded, unsuccessfully, of the Dock Superintendent, the name of the officer responsible for 'this cock and bull story'. He added, quite correctly : 'It is evident that there is an uncommon sense of humour at the London Docks.'

Tusks of ivory and casks of wine have always interested visitors, including, occasionally, Royalty. A Princess, having concluded her visit to the docks, was asked if she would honour the occasion by partaking of a glass of wine. Her Royal Highness was pleased to comment on the expert manner in which the attendant cooper dispensed, direct from the selected cask, the Dock Company's hospitality. Lowering the glass which had barely touched the Royal lips and replacing her veil, she turned to the Dock Superintendent. 'I think that our friend here,' indicating the cooper, 'might be allowed to finish that as a special treat.' The Superintendent hastened to give his permission. Our friend, a member of an ancient craft whose heraldic device could have very fitly been an unmuzzled ox treading out the corn, downed the port.

The next call the Royal party made was to the Spice warehouse where a parcel of nutmegs was being garbled. Sitting on forms round a large table were a dozen old labourers sorting nutmegs to size, a job reserved for men too old for general work. The Princess paused to watch. Suddenly the Dock Superintendent, imagining a lack of respect that the ancient dockers, not having been rehearsed in their part, had no intention of showing, roared at them : 'On your knees, men, on your knees, get down at once.' The pathetic old men, not one under seventy, lowered their rheumatic knees to the warehouse floor and removed their caps as Royalty passed by.

I had arrived at London Docks at a time of transition. The London and India Docks Company, a major predecessor of the PLA, working under the shadow of incorporation, had recruited few staff. The acceptance by the PLA of their considerable responsibilities had coincided with the first output of the new Secondary Schools, the equal of the present-day Grammar Schools. For their staff the PLA set a higher standard than their predecessors. By 1912 a leaven of eager and well-dressed youngsters had invaded the dock offices. Many stayed only long enough to take a look at their older colleagues. Not liking what they saw and thinking, quite incorrectly as it turned out, that they would grow to look like them, they resigned in droves. As I saw the conditions in which I should be expected to work I began to act on the advice to get out. The First War upset my plans.

To the present generation the conditions that I shall describe will seem unacceptable. I can say that not only were they accepted by the pre-1914 staff but they were as good as and often better than those that an untrained youngster could obtain elsewhere. Harsh as they may now seem to have been, the PLA were good employers then, although not until the Second War were the traditional methods of the old Dock Companies finally eradicated. No employer can be censured for not being beyond his age in his treatment of his staff. Since 1945, when fear as the driving force that kept the staff at their work was finally driven out of the dock gates, the PLA have leant over backwards to give them more than a fair deal. I could quote chapter and verse for this.

The general level among the older staff, and they were in the majority, was deplorably low. Many were physically repulsive with scruffy linen, stained coats and untidy beards. They took comfort from occasional nips from bottles kept in their desks; alongside these were packets of fish and chips or bread and cheese. The work they did was of the simplest kind; over the years it had become mechanical. Fortunately for them neither mechanisation nor automation had arrived to make demands on staff that these people could never meet. They kept out of trouble by doing the minimum work; they had never heard of productivity. It was enough to have perfected the art of making a parade of doing nothing when there was nothing doing. Ant-like they passed the hours, having little to say to each other and less to the youngsters whose hostility they could sense. In our own way we returned this. A junior asking for information on a working practice would quite likely get the answer: 'I had to find that out for myself, you'd better do the same.' As late as 1923, on asking a Measurer a technical question on the measurement of teak, I was given the same dusty answer.

For most of the year they were content to remain at their ledgers for five days a week, until seven o'clock. This overtime of three hours was unpaid; each late worker, irrespective of rank, received ninepence tea money. Tea and dripping toast, as I've said, could be had for a penny. At the end of the month each clerk received a golden sovereign for this accumulated tea money, a substantial help with the family budget. In August 1914 I was required to attend the telephone all night. For this I received the princely sum of half a crown as refreshment money.

In spite of the grim surroundings there was an old-world charm about our relations one with another. The youngest clerk was addressed as 'Mister'. Slapdash abbreviations or nicknames were never used. A clerk's Christian name was, rightly, his personal property not to be bandied about by 'the little friends of all the world' that infest modern publicity. Each morning on arrival, an employee shook hands with the clerks in his immediate circle. If, during the day, he went to another part of the large office, this would be treated as an occasion and he shook hands with the appropriate clerk and his colleagues. Before he left at night it was a courtesy to shake hands once more. The First War destroyed this courteous ritual and it was never revived.

I think that the major contrast between the pre-1914 staff and that of today lay in the entire absence of contacts between management and staff. The latter feared and hated the former. In turn the management ignored the staff save as a means of recording clerical transactions. There was no appreciation of junior staff as potential managers, neither was any regard paid to staff morale, of which there was none. The very occasional visits from Head Office officials were met with a sullen silence. 'Keep your head well down until he's gone' was the safe working rule. If you ever talked about getting on in the service, and obviously a few had done so in the past, you were met with a derisory laugh. 'I had those ideas when I was a boy and look at me now.' In those days we did not know the answer.

The staff was divided into two grades, major and minor. The major staff filled the positions in the dock offices. It also supplied the few executive officers in charge of the working departments of the dock, including the technical staff of engineers and dockmasters. The minor staff were more numerous and peopled the many departmental offices scattered around the dock; in its way it was an expert staff responsible for the cargo handling that included ship discharge, craft and warehouse work. Its members ranged from messenger boys to experienced foremen and included craftsmen such as coopers. Very, very few of the minor staff ever got on to the major staff. As a class they were underpaid and their prospects limited. As late as 1950 one of the many Enquiries into dock working commented on the fact that the pay of the supervisory staff was generally lower than that of those they supervised.

On the major staff, life began at sixteen with the Fourth Class Clerk. An early reform of the PLA had abolished a grade even lower and less well paid. Starting at £50 a year the Fourth Class Clerk progressed by annual increments of £10 to a maximum of £120. On this sum he should be able to marry. While waiting for his family to grow up he waited also for promotion to the next grade. As a Third Class Clerk he rose, by the same gradual steps to £170. By this time his family might be off his hands and he could wait with less impatience for promotion to a Second Class Clerk with a yearly maximum of £210. As a matter of diminishing interest to the staff, there was a grade of First Class Clerk who received the princely sum of £5 a week. The retiring age was sixty-five and the staff pyramid, with its broad base, became progressively narrower as it reached its apex. In each main dock office a Principal Clerk, salary £300 a year, reigned supreme as no clerk has done since the end of the First War, nor will ever do again. His power was absolute. After a word with the Staff Manager a delinquent clerk would be advised to seek work elsewhere, advice which he usually took. It is difficult in the late 1960s to realise how expendable junior clerks were fifty years before. Although the salaries I have quoted, and the wages of the minor staff were much lower, would now be impossible to live on, money did then go a very long way. In the opinion of H. G. Wells, looking back on the 'long afternoon of the Edwardian Summer' the working man had never been able to buy so much with so little money.

2

There were only two openings for the clerical grade. Chances of promotion outside the routine kind were minimal. One was promotion to the Special Classification, a grade long since abolished. Realising that the dock type of clerk just would not do in the City, the London and India Docks Company had set out to find the exceptional clerk, neatly dressed and personally clean. After a trial period in the office of the Dock Superintendent, he was given the opportunity to pass a simple test in the Three R's. On passing this and also a more challenging interview, he was accepted as a member of the Special Classification Staff and could say goodbye to the grime and sordidness of the docks. With higher pay and better prospects he was expected to keep his linen and his fingernails clean. Many managed to do this and carved out a career as a City gent. They rightly regarded themselves as the élite of the staff. There was no nonsense in those days about bringing in graduates from a University to occupy higher positions.

Then there was the Warehousekeepers' grade, a term that originated with the Customs and Excise and expressed the duties of these men admirably. At the bottom was the Second Class Assistant Warehousekeeper. Many of these fell by the wayside unable to stand the strain; many were shot down by their senior officers as incompetent. There was no close season to protect the Assistant Warehousekeeper and the system bred a tough and independent type from which the five dock superintendents, the apex of the operative staff pyramid, were selected. Used to standing on their own feet and not looking for support from their superior officers, the Warehousekeepers' grade were the backbone of the Authority's staff and, in the Second War, of the Transportation Branch of the Royal Engineers.

In practice very few reached the top. Owing to periods when recruitment had been heavy there were blocks in promotion that could only be removed by premature retirements. Conversely, some were lucky because they had entered the service after a gap of several years in recruitment and there was virtually no one in their way. For instance, men who came in when recruiting opened up again in 1936, after a long lapse during the years of the Depression, were specially favoured. Because the Surrey Commercial Docks Company had paid higher salaries than the neighbouring dock companies, their staff were, on the amalgamation in 1909, graded in higher ranks than men who had a similar length of service with the London and India Docks Company. The Cinderella of the whole service was the Millwall Docks Company's staff. For years lowly paid by a near bankrupt concern they were happy to take their place on the new staff ladder, conscious that it did, at least in theory, reach the clouds. To my knowledge none of these unfortunate men ever climbed far; this staff, like that of all the original companies, is now extinct.

Not all were able to avoid trouble even by the generally safe method of doing the minimum of work. Increments, by present-day standards derisory, were stopped on slight pretexts. Should a clerk put the parent company to expense he could say good-bye to further increments for several years, or to further promotion if he had already reached the top of his grade. In 1913 I had a fellow clerk, a former employee of the Millwall Docks Company, whose increment had been stopped in 1903 on account of an error which had cost the company about £100. His case was reopened by the PLA four years after their inception. A tardy justice promoted him to be a Third Class Clerk; there was no mention of back increments. An elderly colleague in the office, nearing the retiring age of sixty-five had never got beyond £110 a year. The last increment that would have taken him to his pitiful maximum as a Fourth Class Clerk at £120 a year had been denied him in the 1880s. As he had not reached his maximum he could not be considered for further promotion.

Staff in this invidious position knew better than to hope that a new Pharaoh would arise that knew not Joseph. At some time in the past a Discipline Book had been instituted. This was kept under lock and key by the Dock Superintendent. Every infringement of the code was duly entered by the man's superintendent. This was done on the instructions of the Staff Manager. To make sure that, on transfer to another dock, a member of the staff should still keep this albatross round his neck an 'extract from the Discipline Book' was attached to his personal papers. An error made in early life thus followed a man throughout his career. It was produced by the Staff Manager on each occasion that the man was interviewed for promotion. I have watched this official point out the record of an entry to the chairman of the selection committees at which I have been present. It may well have affected the choice when rival candidates had equal claims. An officer with whom I had served at the West India Docks and who had proved a mainstay of Transportation in the Eighth Army, being decorated for his courage and outstanding technical ability, applied in 1954 for a senior position in the Authority. At the critical stage of the interview the attention of the General Manager was drawn to an entry in the staff records. Keeping a straight face he asked the candidate if it was true that he had, forty years earlier, joined Kitchener's Army without the Authority's permission. Did he realise that this was still a blot on his career? To the discomfiture of the staff moguls the practice of producing the Discipline Book was then and there abolished.

The raw material for the Discipline Book was the Complaints Form, a sheet of foolscap size and known throughout the service, in half fear and half contempt, as a 'half-sheet'. There was in fact some doubt as to the rank that one must attain before being exempt from the lash of the half-sheet. In 1950 a Dock Superintendent was so ill advised as to give a half-sheet to his own Dockmaster, who, as a Master Mariner of many years' service, very properly refused to accept it. The half-sheet wasted no words. It began by stating the precise nature of the complaint, followed by: 'I now call upon you to state in writing your answer to the above complaint.' The basis of this pernicious system, and half-sheets were often wrongly kept by departmental chiefs indefinitely, to be produced as threats as occasion required, was that a man given a half-sheet was always guilty. The drill provided for the complaints form to be submitted through the usual channels to the Staff Manager who would decide whether the complaint was justified. I never knew a case when he decided in favour of the staff. The system was abused in that weak Principals gave their staff half-sheets for technical offences that, had they any guts, they would themselves have shouldered. With a few shining exceptions, respected throughout the service, the officers under whom I worked were a poor lot. The highest praise that could be accorded an aspiring candidate for promotion was an endorsement by his Dock Superintendent: 'Nothing is known against this man.' When things went wrong an infallible formula was applied by the Head Office : 'Who is the officer responsible and what has he got to say?' The Warehousekeepers' grade were content to know that they had always two chances with the management. They could either be wrong or they could be incorrect; they could not hope to be right, or to please everybody for long.

In 1930 during the worst of the Depression, when unemployment was always at one's elbow, I was surprised to see several of my most competent staff seated each before a half-sheet chewing the ends of their pens. 'Well,' I said, 'you do look a happy lot—what's bitten you?' The senior foreman looked up : 'That's all very well, guv'nor, but Mr —— [the Dock Principal] has given us all half-sheets over some bananas and their tallies that are wrong.' Taking the one lying before him I read : 'On May 22nd 1930 you tallied 165 stems of bananas ex *Jamaica Producer*, into LMS rail wagon No. 126778. On arrival at destination only 164 stems out-turned.' There followed the acidulous invitation to state in writing the accused's answer. This was typical of the use to which the disciplinary code had been degraded.

'How on earth could you remember loading one truck out of hundreds and that weeks ago?' I asked. 'That's just the trouble, we can't.' Five of the staff had similarly worded complaints to answer and none of them looked happy. 'For the first time in your lives you are going to be right,' I told them. 'Put down exactly what I say and not a word more nor less.' They sat there with their pens poised as I dictated.

'Sir, on May 22nd I loaded truck No. —— with —— stems of bananas ex *Jamaica Producer*. My tally is correct, the railway tally is wrong.'

These were duly signed and handed back to the Principal Warehousekeeper, an individual for whom I acquired during the five years that I was his assistant, the greatest contempt. He, I'm sure,

13

knew the inspiration for this unprecedented defence. It did nothing to improve our relations which could not have sunk lower.

One morning, immediately before the First War, one of my then colleagues at the East India Dock had arrived at the main departmental office at the West India Docks. As a new entrant to the service he was surprised to find the usually tame staff in an uproar. No attempt to get out the ledgers for the day's work had been made. The staff were laughing and shouting across the large office; the younger ones were practising some of the new ragtime steps. Even the sedate Principal Clerk was chatting amiably with two senior colleagues and beaming on the disorder all round. My friend was immediately grabbed by two of the older staff. 'Haven't you heard? The old Bogey Man died suddenly last night.'

The high official whose sudden but long-awaited demise had now sent a peal of joy from London Bridge to distant Tilbury was the Staff Inspector of the PLA. A job such as this, with its duties ill defined, had, in the hands of the late occupant, become a menace to all and sundry. Many were the tales told of this super-snooper, this forerunner of the Gestapo. Allowing for exaggeration by the staff, whose belief that while there's death there's hope had now been justified, little good could be said of him; his job was not filled.

This was the Gradgrind mentality that permeated the staff from the higher rungs of the ladder down to the newly joined messenger boy. The buck was passed until it could go no lower. No official accepted responsibility that he could by any means, however shady, pass on to his junior. No official would have been commended by his colleagues had he done so. Co-operation or any form of joint effort within the staff was non-existent. In 1912 a feeble Staff Association damned by Head Office encouragement, was in the last stage of dying of inanition.

If these were the conditions in which the staff worked how much worse were those of the port labour. Dismissals for breach of discipline were instantaneous and there was no appeal. No attempt was made to understand the point of view of men labouring with few or no amenities, in the vilest of weather, on monotonous and often ill-paid jobs without hope of bettering their conditions. In the 1930s some latrines for labourers in the older docks had not advanced beyond a pole suspended over a trough. Some offices still had earth closets until the Second War. To be made a permanent labourer at twenty-one was the height of good fortune; to remain on this grade until seventy was the only prospect. The maximum benevolent allowance given to a labourer with 'fifty years of undetected crime' was ten shillings a week. With the labour market as it stood before 1914 this was considered to be good. During a labour dispute of this period I overheard an officer, who, a few years later was solely responsible for the operational work in all the docks, offer his well-thought-out solution: 'Put them up against the wall and shoot them.'

Since those good old days the PLA, in common with other progressive employers, have seized on their incoming staff as material capable of being trained and tested for later positions of high responsibility. Junior clerks are now regarded as potential managerial timber. The business of running a port demands a lifetime's study and to be capable in time of solving major problems needs all the encouragement and support from his superior officers that the latter can give. It is perhaps wrong to censure a corporation for not being in advance of its own times. A system that gave encouragement to the bogey-man type of executive (and the official Staff Inspector was only a little worse than those not so titled) had its repercussions on the efficiency of the whole organisation. Dock knowledge, slowly acquired, was closely valued by its owners. It formed their mental capital not to be dissipated nor even shared, save with those few who had more than you.

How then would staff conditioned by such methods have responded to the mechanical revolution that swept the ports after 1945? The answer is that they would have clung so tenaciously to their small technical knowledge, despite its pending obsolescence, as to make progress of any kind impossible. As late as 1954 the surging tide of mechanisation was stayed at a major dock pending the retirement of a Dock Superintendent known to have little enthusiasm for new methods of handling cargo. It was fortunate that new ideas did not come until the Second War had made a clean sweep of men 'who had never done it that way before'.

3

My release from the dreary job of examining passes was now due.
Summoned peremptorily to the private room of the Principal
Examiner, my polite 'Good morning, sir' was met with a very
definite chill. Without a word, a pass for Joel's van with fifty bags
of onions, was pushed in my face. My initials had been placed
prominently in red ink over the load line of the pass. This indicated
my complete satisfaction with the transaction.

The pass was unsigned. It was a blank cheque and I had honoured it. In doing so I had brought shame to my own cloth and to
the Examiners' staff. No longer was I worthy to be numbered
among the elect. I had given zest to the gibe incessantly hurled at
our select tribe, 'tick, trust and tremble'. I had now reached the
third state. It turned out to be the best day's work I ever left un-
done. With the minimum publicity I was demoted to the Gas and
Water Department, also in London Dock. The accepted practice
was observed and the unfortunate constable on the gate was left
to carry the can.

In those far-off days simple jobs were done in a simple way. In
a small office on Tower Hill an officer known as the Comptroller
sat, and with a small staff, looked after the finances of the PLA. He
told Lord Devonport how much there was in the kitty and how
much he could spend. What more does the present vast machine
do? It was the same with the Gas and Water Department which
had recently taken over Electric Light and Power, but with no
extra staff. Supplies for each of the five dock controls came through
main gas and water meters. Of the quantity supplied not all was
used by the PLA; much was metered to tenants of the docks. A
simple sum each week produced the net usage by the Authority.

Each clerk on the department was responsible for his allotted dock. He was familiar with the position there of every meter and it was his business to follow the work going on in the dock, as it affected, particularly, water consumption. This was so in the case of contractors working on new buildings. Many millions of gallons of fresh water were also metered to ships. There were even water barges that hawked water round to ships where no quay meters were available. Quarterly accounts were rendered by the department to the many hundreds of tenants who used gas, water and electricity. The simple system of checking main and subsidiary consumption enabled a close watch to be kept on waste or excessive use. By comparing readings at the time and on the spot, one was expected to investigate immediately abnormal consumption; yet another example of the good husbandry that was instilled into the pre-1914 staff. Shortly before my arrival on the department the palm for diligence had been awarded to a clerk who had detected an attempt to obtain large quantities of water without payment. When supplied to a contractor for some new works at the Royal Docks, the portable meter stood at 850,000 gallons. A week later it read 875,000 gallons, an apparent consumption of a mere 25,000 gallons. Checking back to the appropriate main meter the clerk found that over 300,000 gallons had to be accounted for and there was no other substantial tenant in the area served by the main meter. On being pressed the contractor admitted that his men might have been careless in attaching the meter to the supply stand. It might, in fact, have been run backward. What had taken place was that the meter had been allowed to register from 850,000 to its capacity of 1,000,000 gallons. It had then been detached and run backwards to 850,000 gallons, refitted correctly and an innocuous 25,000 gallons recorded as the consumption for the week. A commendatory entry in the records of the Staff Department was duly made; as this clerk was pensioned on his then rank it is difficult to see how this did him any good.

Apart from one's home control each clerk was expected to take over the work during annual leave or sickness of any of his colleagues. To uncover and to clean the meters, many of which were in pits, the Engineer's department provided a labourer who came round and helped in a dozen ways. I was fortunate in having as my early bear leader, a foreman, Bill Lambert, who was the most trusted man on the department. He knew, I think, everything that was worth knowing about the docks and the River Thames and the ships that used them.

'What's that bucket for, tied up to the mast of that ship over there?' I would ask.

'That means that the ship wants the water barge. You can see that she's on a buoy berth and that's the only way to fill her fresh water tanks.'

'Why has somebody tied a knot in the flag that ship's flying?'

'She wants the Customs, that's why. Perhaps she wants to change her bar stocks.'

I soon became knowledgeable on ship and tug funnels; I learnt to recognise the flags of every nation's vessels and even the house markings of the different lighterage companies. Dockers, I found, had a language of their own. 'Up and down' if you asked the time meant the full hour. A 'plumper' referred to a package that had scaled at the exact number of hundredweights. The 'ceiling' of a ship or a barge was the floor. A term that seemed to have more than one use and whose origin it took me several years to discover was 'greenacre'. When a set of cargo had come adrift whilst being landed and its contents had spewed over the quay, it made a greenacre. Similarly a man could make a greenacre of a job as I had done over Joel's pass a few years before. The application of the term (it is still in use but cannot long survive the introduction of container traffic) is still faithful to its origin. In 1836 a shady Londoner, Mr Greenacre, met a washerwoman, Hannah Brown. She could have been no ordinary washerwoman for she convinced Greenacre that she owned £400, a useful sum in those days. He promptly proposed marriage, his fourth, was accepted and the wedding was fixed for Christmas Day at St Giles Church in Camberwell. On Christmas Eve he murdered her. Faced with the disposal of the body he argued that what was certainly difficult as a unit might be more easily performed in stages. Parts of the body of the unfortunate Hannah Brown were buried in separate places on the outskirts of London. As he sat in one of the early horse buses on his way to bury the head of the unfortunate woman at Chalk Farm, he is said to have remarked to a fellow passenger, while fondling the parcel on his knees: 'I ought by rights to be paying two fares.' The remark passed but it was remembered by a woman passenger whose evidence at the subsequent trial was damning. He was arrested early in 1837 and was hanged on May 3rd. His trial caused so much interest that seats at the Central Criminal Court fetched £1 each.

The incident figured in the broadsheets of the period. The docker with his ready wit saw the implication and adopted the term. In the late 1920s, on the morning of the execution of the Ilford murderer, Bywaters, I was walking along the deck of a ship at the East India Dock. In front of me a set of bags of sugar came out of the hold; one bag hung by the neck, kept in position by only one leg of the rope sling. The winchdriver, knowing my feelings about badly made-up sets, made to lower it on the deck. The hatchwayman, who had his back to me, called out: 'That's all right, let old Bywaters go.' Macabre but very topical.

Each dock in those days had its own flavour; changes in fashion, the demand for raw materials and commercial practices have altered much of this and destroyed the colour and the smell. Firstly London Dock, where you picked your way over cobblestones that harassed the feet, through narrow lanes between hundreds of wine casks, laid out for gauging, and its many miles of vaults. Fruit came from the Mediterranean, onions, lead and quicksilver from Spain. Spices of all kinds and ivory in large tusks came by barge from ships discharging in the Lower Docks. Nearer home, tinplates came by coaster from South Wales and Guinness stout from Dublin. A deadly piece of dynamite, unrecognised then for its potential menace to the port industry, was carried by these small Irish packet ships—Jacobs' biscuits, in five feet cube heavy boxes, the prototype container.

St Katharine Docks lay on the other side of Nightingale Lane where James I had hunted a stag three centuries before. Bastille-like warehouses, their fronts flush with the dock quay, were grouped in light-excluding squares around its two water areas. There was no avoiding the pungent smell of hops in oversized 'pockets' from Bremen, or the greasy smell of bales of wool that were incessantly rattled over the cobbles on hand trucks. The penetrating scent of essential oils came from the dock premises of a tenant; the rich smells of China and Indian teas were wafted from a nearby warehouse. It was truly said that a man could, blindfold, locate himself anywhere in this control, by his nose. Within a few yards was the full panorama of the Pool, with Tower Bridge raising its twin bascules to the Belle steamers with their load of passengers for Margate or Clacton.

Apart from the safe thrills to a young boy within the twenty-foot-high dock walls there was the excitement of finding short cuts through the back streets of Wapping and Shadwell. The vast rookery that had ministered to the many wants of sailors, paid off from the long voyages of the sailing vessels, was then in its decline. The Blitz of the Second War destroyed it completely. Many were the tales, often certainly true, told by the older clerks, of the domestic industries that fringed the main dock gates. That it was an area where women's work was never done could, even then, be glimpsed from the staid pages of the Authority Bye Laws. Herein access to the dock was forbidden to 'pimps, ponces and prostitutes'. I never walked down the nearby Artichoke Hill nor St John's Hill without visualising the morning-after feeling of the sailor, stripped even of his clothes and robbed certainly of his accumulated pay and thrown out into the gutter. It was said that the Victorian police were lenient provided that the common decencies were observed. A piece of brown paper made fast with string, round the man's middle satisfied both sides, if not the victim.

Not only was the night life of Wapping able to attract the sailor home from the sea, but it competed successfully with the sicker appeal of the gas-lit West End. Patronised by Edward, Prince of Wales, it flourished until the regular schedules kept by steamships and the payment of crews through the City offices of the companies destroyed the income of the bordello and the gaming parlour. However, Royalty left their mark. In the early 1900s the old fish market at Shadwell was cleared and a pleasant little park laid out on the river front. When it was named the 'King Edward Memorial Park' the inhabitants had reason to feel that tradition had been served and a fragrant memory perpetuated. From the main gate of London Docks ran the Ratcliffe Highway, long the Regent Street of sailors from the Seven Seas. Not only could they buy any articles or service desired, but Jamrach's famous animal shops were waiting to buy from them the strange and exotic animals and birds that had survived the rigours of the voyage home. I remember passing these two dusty and rather evil-smelling shops from which came the eldritch shrieks of parrots and monkeys

Left On entering the
PLA in 1912.
Right Out of the Line—
France, January 1916.

Shadwell Basin, London Dock, with the fine church of St George's in the East, in the background.

among the more easily recognised sounds. Jamrach's have long since gone out of business and their premises destroyed.[1]

Next in order came the Surrey Commercial Docks. This, by good luck, was my new home ground. I little thought that nearly forty years later I should return there as the Superintendent of the Docks. In 1951 I was amused to see the main gas meter just inside the Main Entrance in Rotherhithe Road, still in position and untouched by two major wars. Reading the meters at this dock was a leisurely chore that took all day Friday, Saturday morning and late into the afternoon. Saturday was, until 1920, a normal working day and a half-day was only by favour of one's Principal. Before starting on the Saturday amble round the quieter parts of the dock, the Engineer's labourer and I would call at Mrs Challis' coffee shop. Here on scrubbed tables and seated on wooden forms we would enjoy our mug of sweet coffee and slabs of margarine and toast for the absurd sum of twopence. As I had walked from London Docks via Ratcliffe Highway and the Rotherhithe Tunnel I felt justified in squandering the bus fare we were allowed.

The Surrey Commercial Docks had a distinct character. Alone among the enclosed docks of the port it had thrived on softwood, Canadian produce and bulk grain. The dock was always a law unto itself; as the Dock Superintendent as late as 1951 I became immediately conscious that I was king in my own castle there.

Most of the dock area was given over to softwood timber ships from the Baltic and White Sea ports. Before 1914 many were still driven by sail. From Tower Bridge one could catch a glimpse from the top of the horse-drawn bus of a forest of masts. For many years one berth was retained for ships bringing cargoes of ice. This was in large 'pigs' and was landed by steel scissors on to the vans of the United Carlo Gatti Company. How else could one have ice before the days of domestic refrigerators? Timber was handled, and it still is, by dealporters, one of the remaining specialist classes of port labour. In those days there were several thousand of these men who worked hard, drank heavily and were too old at forty. A fascinating part of the dock lay in the Lavender and Acorn area where large shallow ponds, of many acres, provided floating storage for large logs of pitch pine and Oregon pine. To cope with

[1] A picture of the shops as I knew them appears in Thornbury's *Old and New London*—that mine of information on forgotten London.

this traffic there was a staff of rafters, staff men who were assisted by casual labourers who had gained some skill. Walking across the dock, hopping from one raft on to the end log of its neighbour was an art, and acquired only after several bootfuls of dock water. In those days the river was comparatively free from industrial pollution and there were no oil slicks floating on the dock waters. Fish abounded in the timber ponds. The Surrey Docks Company had allowed fishing, for a small charge, and week-end anglers lined the banks. The Company had also maintained a thriving swimming club. Each year an open-air gala took place in a water space cleared of timber. It says much for the cleanliness of the river water that it was possible for this event to be held, from 1923, in the West India Docks, until growing pollution put an end to it in the middle 1930s.

The India and Millwall Docks were similar to the London and St Katharine Docks. The warehouses were larger and grimmer, the transit sheds bigger and the ship tonnage ran into thousands of tons. The PLA did the ship discharge and it was a fine sight to stand at the end of either main quay and to watch the endless movement of cargo from the many ships and the incessant shifting of craft that accompanied this. The East India Dock, the home of the Honourable East Indian Company, was a busy part of the dock control. Both the North Quay and parts of the East India Dock were then being modernised with the demolition of jetties and the building of new brick sheds. Millwall Docks, like the Surrey, kept its own flavour for many years after the amalgamation. The former dock was itself in a ramshackle state; dozens of small sheds littered the area. It was said with some truth that the only building policy the dock company had was to put up another small shed whenever the yearly accounts showed a surplus of a few hundred pounds. Uneconomical to run, they each held only a handful of cargo; there was a general air of being rundown about the dock and this persisted until the major improvements interrupted by the Second War.

The Royal Albert and Victoria Docks (the building of the King George V Dock had only recently commenced) were a treasure house to a romantic boy. There were ships of the P & O Line, spewing out returned missionaries and choleric colonels, with their foreign-looking baggage, bamboo chairs and Benares brass trays.

Native crews from Bengal and the Punjab slopped about the quays on their way to the native latrines or, stripped to a loin-cloth, would stand on a wintry day on the deck of their ship dowsing their bodies from a small can of water. Apart from some frozen meat in the cold stores, tobacco in the special warehouses and bulk grain in Victoria Dock this huge control was entirely a transit dock, where eighty per cent of the incoming cargoes went overside into barges for dispersal to the river wharves and to the upper docks of the PLA. Apart from Far East traffic this was the home of the larger North American ships. The s.s. *Minnewaska* of the Atlantic Transport Line was then the largest ship to berth so close to London itself. In 1939 the *Mauretania* of Cunard fame made an initial entry into this control but the war prevented her regular run there.

Tilbury Dock was kept as a prize for a good boy. The meters were read by the senior clerk who did not lightly hand over his job to a junior. Overnight preparation for the task was made by drawing a rail voucher, to be presented at Fenchurch Street Station of the Southend and Tilbury Section of the Midland Railway. The 8.13 a.m. disentangled itself from the suburbs before it reached Barking and ambled into the open country, stopping at stations with romantic names like Dagenham, Rainham, Purfleet and Tilbury Town. The latter was the home of many of the staff and most of the dockers. In the pierhead area the East and West India Docks Company had built a really good hotel and two terraces of 'Officers' Houses' where lived the Dock Superintendent, the Engineer, the Dockmaster and other high officials of the company. Being twenty-six miles from London Bridge and with the railway its only link with the City, Tilbury Docks lived in a world of its own. All traffic was handled by rail or craft. None of the staff in those days had cars; the highest of the dock or shipping company's officials walked round on foot as their predecessors had done. Tilbury Docks was a riot of colour with its native crews even more varied than those in the Royal Docks; there were few ships that were not crewed by natives. The P & O, the Orient, Bibby's and the City Line produced the many castes of India whilst one could detect from the Ben Line the little men from the Malay Archipelago or Mongols from northern China.

Part of the excitement of Tilbury Docks was the superb view of the River Thames from the Entrance Lock and the Basin. Better

23

still, if on a fine afternoon, with an hour to spare before the London-bound train, one could find a sheltered spot on the river bank, below Tilbury Station and near the old Tilbury Fort. Here in comfort you could watch a panorama of shipping not to be seen elsewhere in the world. Whatever the state of the tide ships were edging their way past the reporting station at Gravesend on the opposite side of the river. Some had dropped anchor to await their time of entry into the docks. Others almost as large were pushing their way up-river with the incoming tide to arrive at the Royal Docks so as to enter on that tide. Everywhere there was a swirl of smaller ships and tugs, with the distinctive Thames sailing barge, now almost extinct, by the dozen. Single dumb barges heaved over into the Tilbury Basin, propelled by a lone lighterman hauling on his sweeps, a sight that has long since disappeared. It was not easy to settle down again in the office at London Docks, booking up meter readings and making out accounts. If life here tended to become monotonous there was always the great event of the month to which one looked forward and in which one could humbly participate. It had long been recognised by the dock companies that the act of paying people—handing them the money—was and always would be a dead-horse job. The sooner it was over the sooner could staff get back to productive work. My principal was a First Class Clerk, a dignified figure in a frock coat, and to him had been deputed the paying, on the last day of the month, of the clerks on the Examiner's staff of the London and St Katharine Docks. On the morning he would arrive in his best frock coat and an added air of importance that plainly meant that he had no time to discuss routine matters. Absenting himself from his desk at an early hour he would return later in the morning with the correct number of envelopes, each bearing the name of a clerk and the amount to which he was entitled. These would be arranged in their correct order of seniority in a large tray on his desk. When he was satisfied that everything had been done in a seemly and decent order, he would turn to the nearest clerk with the order: 'If any of the gentlemen have arrived, tell them, please, that I am ready for them.' Thus was preserved the fiction that no gentleman would show undue haste in drawing his salary, although we all knew that the first dozen were champing at the bit in the outer office. By lunch-time the ceremony was almost complete. It remained only for we juniors to approach the dwindling pile, each to receive and to sign for, his monthly payment of £4 3s. 4d. (in golden sovereigns and real silver), less Lloyd George's insurance deductions.

This was the picture of London's dockland seen through the eyes of a very junior clerk whose leisure time was spent in an attempt to get away from it all. In November 1914 I should have taken the examination for an Officer of HM Customs and Excise. In September of that year I joined an Infantry Battalion of the London Regiment of Territorials. When I returned to the Gas and Water Department in 1919 it had established itself under the arches at Crutched Friars.

4

When I had applied to the Head Office during the summer of 1912 the entry to the building had been blocked by a queue that stretched round into St Mary Axe. The fear that these were competitors for the clerical position for which I was to be interviewed was soon corrected by the janitor who guarded the door. He told me that they were ex-strikers who were soliciting the privilege of a 'B' ticket for work in place of the permanency that they had forfeited. I had known that there had been a strike but here, before my career in the port had officially begun, was physical evidence of the struggle between labour and the port employers that was to occupy so much of my working time and to be a lasting source of interest.

As I settled down in my job and talked to some of the older staff I learnt that the strike of 1912 was the third of the major stoppages that the port of London had seen during the last quarter of a century. The outbreak of 1889—I had heard my father, a lifelong Liberal, talk admiringly of John Burns and the part he had played in this—had set the pattern. From the archives to which I had subsequent access in the Head Office I was able to put together the happenings of the years that had preceded the outbreak of the First War. I came to understand the parts played by the major actors, some of whom were still alive and active, and how this phase fitted into the long history of labour in the docks of London.

In August 1889 Ben Tillet asked the East and West India Docks Company to raise the pay of the dockers he represented, from 5d. to 6d. an hour, with 8d. an hour for overtime pay and a guaranteed four hours' engagement. The practice of the times allowed foremen to take on labour for as little as half an hour's work so this was indeed a revolutionary demand which the dock company promptly rejected. They also turned down the men's request that contractors should be dismissed and the work done by direct piecework arrangements with the dock company's officials, an improvement that was long overdue. The men had not a good word to say about the contractors. They were employed by the Dock Superintendent to carry out the normal work of discharging or loading ships or doing the warehouse work. They did all this for an agreed rate per ton and by alternate slave driving and cajolery, with always a surplus of labour to play with, made a very good profit. It was the normal thing for the contractor to pay his labour in a dockside pub, in whose profits he was interested. When there was no work there was always beer for the regulars, chalked up on the slate, against earnings to come. As public houses had not, in those days, any closing hours, many of the slender payments that the contractors made found their way back into his pocket. Dealporters, many of them from Ireland, made up their own family gangs. The ganger hired the gang out to the contractors; he paid the members what he considered enough to keep them working and in beer. Few men were brave or foolish enough to fight the family for what they considered to be their rightful earnings. No wonder that the more responsible of the casuals saw in piecework a fair return for individual work. After the strike of 1889 there was indeed an increase in the small amount of dock work considered suitable to be done on piecework. The contractors were gradually eliminated from the docks, the last of them, the timber pilers, lingering until the 1920s at the Surrey Commercial Docks.

The dock companies used contractors because it saved their overhead costs for paying men and supervising their work. A docker of those days said of them: 'They grow fat on our work. They spend the best part of their time in the public houses, coming round occasionally to swear at us or to bully us. They treat us more like dogs than men. They will only engage men who "stand treat" or who are ready to liquor them up.' In the daily newspapers of 1889 one can read of the hard grinding life of the London docker. Against the stringency imposed on the casual as normal routine, there came occasionally the day when a full day's pay brought joy to his family, and 'then the frying pan is brought out of the cupboard and a family feast begins'. It is pathetic how often the frying pan as a symbol of prosperity appears in the Press of that period.

Ben Tillet, a labourer in the service of the East and West India Docks Company, had already had a limited success in organising labour. At his place of work he had formed a local union called the Tea Operatives and General Labourers Association. Throughout the five gruelling weeks that the strike lasted he led the ever-increasing army of strikers and proved that he was a thorough and competent organiser of men. He was helped by contributions from the public, workers in the Dominions, particularly Australia, as well as the growing body of trade unionists in this country.

At no time in the history of the docks in London had the proprietory companies been in a more vulnerable position. After their disastrous building of Tilbury Docks, the East and West India Docks Company was virtually bankrupt and had been glad to accept the very unfavourable merger offered by the London and St Katharine Docks Company. This produced the London and India Docks Joint Committee. It had been in existence for only eight months when Ben Tillet led 2,500 men from their work in the East, West and South West India Docks. By August 16th casual men at the Royal Albert and Victoria Dock, and even those from distant Tilbury, withdrew their labour. Tillet and six labourers were invited to the Head Office of the Joint Committee to meet the Chairman, a Mr Norwood. In an age when Mr Gradgrind was typical of City directors, Mr Norwood, from all accounts, was a very fair and reasonable employer. His conduct over the five weeks that the strike lasted, and during the distressing period that followed its settlement, seems, in spite of a bad Press, defection of his allies and personal insult and provocation, to have been that of a man humanely in advance of his time. When the strike started he was a sick man; he died shortly after it was settled.

Although some progress was made on the initial talks on piece-work and contractors, no advance on the basic rate was possible. It would have cost the Joint Committee an additional £100,000 a year, a prohibitive sum to a concern already carrying a near bankrupt company. The offer to pay the men the additional penny per hour, provided that the shipping companies, the main customers of the docks, would accept increased charges, was turned down without any discussion by the latter. On August 20th, 3,500

28

men left work at the Surrey Commercial Docks; on the same day the entire staff of seventy men responsible for housing the fabulously valuable cargoes stored at the Joint Committee's Uptown Warehouses came out in support of the strikers. This was indeed a tactical blow for it meant that cargoes from the Far East that could be discharged in the Lower Docks by blackleg labour would have to remain in the dock sheds to the great embarrassment of the City merchants and the Crown who risked a loss of revenue in the disturbed conditions of the times.

The strike was now front-page news. At this stage John Burns, the man whose name (in spite of political services that lasted until 1914) was always to be associated with the struggle for the Dockers' Tanner, came into the picture. Now he took over from Tillet the tactical direction of the strike; he harangued the men, kept their hopes going by skilful promises of jam tomorrow, visited the dock gate pickets by hansom cab from six o'clock each morning, and took time off to attend the funeral of a docker—'the poor fellow had died of semi-starvation'. In the short space of three weeks he became a demi-god; strikers' wives brought their babies into the streets as he passed, for him to kiss. His control of the undisciplined strikers was superb and also relentless. He commanded 'For God's sake keep your heads clear and don't go and do anything rash', and his command was obeyed. He had a superb physique and a powerful voice, an asset in pre-microphone days. As a ship's engineer he had knocked about the world. In 1887 he had served a sentence of six weeks' imprisonment for resisting the police at a Trafalgar Square meeting.

A strike of this size, at least 15,000 dockers were involved during the first few days, soon began to get out of hand. With hunger the main ally of the employers it was necessary to keep the genuine strikers occupied and contented. The idea of a daily march had an immediate appeal. The strikers, by showing themselves to the public, could collect money from them, particularly in a sympathetic City and West End—the need for this was urgent. As the daily procession started from the area of the London Docks it was routed to pass the head offices of the hated Joint Committee in Leadenhall Street. The behaviour of the dockers was restrained throughout the weeks that the processions continued, although a timorous Press announced that 'some firms have placed all their valuables in the keeping of their bankers'.

Burns and Tillet were directly responsible for the discipline of the strikers. At no time did they lose the sympathy of the public. This was important because the leaders had, somehow, in the absence of a union strike fund, to find enough money to prevent the striking dockers from returning to work. Many were kept busy picketing the dock entrances; for this each received two shillings a day. The job was no sinecure. The few hundred permanent men were still at work. Volunteer or blackleg labour was drifting down to the docks attracted by the generous offer of permanent employment that the Joint Committee held out. During the time that the strike lasted free board and lodging were also provided. The pickets earned their daily pittance. At all costs blacklegs were to be discouraged. With their excellent local knowledge, small and determined groups rushed from one gate to another whilst inside the Customs fence a few terrified men, intent on escaping with their day's earnings, searched for an unguarded gate. The police were powerless to stop this intimidation. The Home Secretary undertook to deal suitably with such incidents as were brought officially to his notice. Meanwhile some 12,000 pickets continued to terrorise a few hundred blacklegs. The challenge issued by the Directors that all the volunteer labour needed to keep the docks working could be had if the pickets were withdrawn was ignored by Burns who kept his combat troops active for the five weeks that the strike lasted. In any case this unsavoury business was taking place within the purlieus of dockland; the attention and the contributions of the public were concentrated on the orderly march that daily wound its way through the City to Hyde Park. Burns publicly deprecated cases of extreme violence when he was forced to notice them. 'Superintendents and the clerical staff', the Press reported, 'carry revolvers for self-protection, they have been so constantly threatened.'[1] Of the 1,000 men the Joint Committee sought to engage in one week within the dock, only 300 dared to remain, although they were offered 21s. a week plus their food and shelter. Blackleg labour was, in fact, the one weapon that would

---

[1] I have discussed conditions during the Great Strike of 1889 with many who served throughout this period but I have not heard of an issue of firearms by the Joint Committee to its staff.

break the strike and Burns could not compromise on this issue. He quickly realised the futility of parading hungry dockers through the West End whilst blacklegs with well-filled stomachs were working uninterruptedly in the East End. To Mr Norwood's telegraphed message that 'John Burns has ordered 60,000 strikers to get the men out at all the docks and puts full responsibility on the Directors' the Home Secretary made no response. The dock police continued to guard the gates, the blacklegs went to ground and the strike went on.

From the start Burns knew that he must get more and more money to keep the strike going. The daily march with its registered collectors (paid 2s. a day attracted showers of money, mainly in coppers. Large donations were needed and these had to be sponsored by the Press and the Pulpit. To secure this support Burns put over the idea that he was fighting labour's battle and the world was invited to admire—and to pass the hat round. £150 was collected the first week, to be followed by a bumper offering of £80—large sums in those days. Burns opened an account at the Poplar branch of the London and South Western Bank, and scrupulous accounts were kept. A procession through the West End brought in over £300. Other unions showed their solidarity with the dockers in practical form. Before the strike was a week old the Shipwrights Provident Union offered £100 and the Council of the Gas Stokers sent £50. The Coopers Union gave practical expression to their motto 'Love as Brethren' by sending along the same amount. A symptom of the support that was generally felt for the dockers was the opening of a Lord Mayor's Fund which brought in £1,600.

The strike would, however, have collapsed without the truly magnificent support it received from Australian labour. Week after week promises and money were telegraphed from the dock workers in the Australian ports. Melbourne alone sent £4,000; it was subsequently revealed that some £24,000 had been received from the strikers' fellow workers in the Australian continent. This was more than half the total sum subscribed from all sources.

The momentum of the strike was sustained not only by the cash value of these offerings. Each new day Burns had to face a crowd of hungry dockers who looked to him and to Tillet for good news. The obduracy of the Directors did not provide a single titbit of encouragement to the ragged army that had begun to look over its shoulders to the dock gates and the promise of work. Burns was indeed fortunate. Each new day he was able to announce a fresh promise of help—a telegraphed £1,000 from Adelaide or a further £1,500 from Sydney. After the strike was over Burns admitted that his arithmetic had, at times, been weak and that the line that separated promises from actual receipts had become blurred.

How was all this money spent? Despite newspaper cavilling about the cost of flags and banners, there was never any doubt that the fund was properly administered. Printed food tickets were issued in lieu of money, and there was no reason to doubt Burns' later statement that 'in no single instance have men in our union had less than 10s. a week in strike pay'. Private charity helped. General Booth, in the early flush of his evangelical success in darkest London, ordered his soup kitchens and his cheap food depots in East London to supply penny meals at half price to the strikers' families. Mrs Gladstone, on her way to the Continent, found time to visit the relief arrangements made by a kindly vicar at Blackwall. The undoubted privations among the men were reduced by the adjustments and improvisations that cushioned the shock of the lost wages. Household furniture was pawned until a box and a kitchen table spelt luxury. The lodging houses and the hostels of the East End suffered heavily. The threepenny supper and the bed that these places provided had satisfied the normal needs of the casual worker; the nightly bed was the first luxury to go. 'It is our Bill who has come home to sleep whilst the strike lasts' was the explanation given to neighbours inquisitive at the advent of a new face.

Whilst Burns and Tillet were encouraged by the money that poured in from distant parts, Burns was disappointed at the American response. He confided to a meeting at the dock gates 'whereas the Australians had responded to their appeal, their brother workmen in America had treated them with a lot of long-winded sentiments, but as for spondulicks and dollars, they had not given a single cent'. Burns and Tillet were also becoming embarrassed by workers in other industries who insisted on joining in the fight. Correctly discerning that the purpose of the struggle would quickly be lost in the welter of striking miners, gas workers and those in the distributive trades, Burns advised them to go back to their work. Already the strike had put up the cost of living. Despite the acrimony and the physical brutality caused by the employment of a few hundred volunteers, output from the docks had dropped to a trickle. Among the first men to leave work were the stevedores, the men who loaded and discharged ships—the aristocrats of dockland. The lightermen and the carmen had also withdrawn their labour. In a port where some eighty per cent of incoming cargoes were discharged overside to craft and where there was a sizable loading of ships from craft alongside, this sufficed to paralyse the port, a paralysis that no amount of volunteer labour could cure.

5

When it was seen that the struggle was going to be a long one and that victory for the employers was by no means certain, a Saturnalia of strikes broke out. Many were caused by the loss of work that followed on the closing down of the docks; ship scrapers, soapworkers from Silvertown, orange porters from the wharves and 6,000 men from the Thames Ironworks, the only remaining shipbuilding works in London, all came out. They were joined by the girls employed at Frost Brothers Rope Works. Not all of them were dependent entirely on the docks; the strike fever soon lost all contact with the struggle maintained day after day by Burns. The surprising feature of this industrial sideline was the almost instant concessions made by the employers to the several demands of their workpeople. Such was the alarm and despondency that had spread among the employing classes. Meanwhile the dockers struggled on, now unimpeded by their unwanted allies. Small wonder that the timorous saw it as the dreaded fight between Capital and Labour. By the end of August many of the Thames wharfingers were certain that there was a Communist under every bed. One of them described the position as 'determined and possibly pre-arranged struggles on the part of organised labour to secure better terms of the capitalist employer'. Memories of the Paris Commune of 1871 were still active.

Both the stevedores and the lightermen remained with the dockers until the end.

The struggle was now in its third week. Well-meant but unsuccessful efforts had been made almost daily to bring agreement between the two parties. The Directors were willing to consider working hours and terms of engagement, even to giving way on the contractors. Only on the dockers' tanner were they adamant.

To Burns was given a vision of what actually did happen on a May morning in 1926 when labour solidly ceased work and set in motion the General Strike. If chaos could be made to overtake the daily life of London, all this could be conveniently put at Mr Norwood's door and that of his co-Directors. The General Committee of the strike issued on August 30th, 1889 the following imposing Manifesto. They 'solemnly appealed to the workers of all grades and of every calling, to refuse to go to work on Monday, September 2nd, unless the Directors have, before noon on Saturday, frankly and fully conceded the demands of the strikers'. The document finished on a rather unctuous note : 'Our studied moderation has been mistaken by our ungenerous opponents for lack of courage and want of resources.'

The reception given to this remarkable document was immediately hostile. The Press quickly pounced on its weak point : 'Mr Burns and his friends are to hold up a finger and four million people are to be subjected to discomfort immeasurable and loss incalculable.' If Londoners were to be held to ransom by one of the parties in a dispute, the rights and wrongs of which few understood and fewer still cared about, that would be the end of the practical sympathy that many had shown. The strikers were faced with a worried week-end. At Dock House, the Joint Committee's headquarters, the Acting Lord Mayor and Cardinal Manning[1] had debated the issue during Saturday but had wisely refrained from issuing a statement. The general feeling was expressed in a few words : 'The Manifesto has fallen flat, it would cover its authors with ridicule if it failed and public reprobation if it succeeded.' Late on the Saturday night it was withdrawn by the strike committee; the workers of London were invited instead to double their efforts to support the strikers and their families.

On the employers' side during the five weeks that the strike lasted there was a distressing lack of cohesion. The wharfingers had already begun to flirt with the men's leaders, offering them terms that Burns realised would have been repudiated had the strike within the docks failed. If the wharves could have got back to normal working they would have secured much of the traffic

[1] There has always been a strong element of Irish Catholics among dock-workers in the East End of London.

that had hitherto used the docks and traffic lost is always hard to regain. Three wharves only were successful and they conceded the full demands of the men.

The Achilles' heel in the surprisingly efficient organisation built up by Burns and Tillet was, from the first, the stevedores of the Surrey Commercial Docks. These men made a very tight pocket of specialist labour that enjoyed a monopoly of the discharge of timber ships. Their conditions and their outlook were superior to those of the workers on the north side of the river and they had, very early on, formed the 'South Side Council of the Labour Protection League'. This body was not unresponsive to overtures from their employers, the master stevedores, where the relations between the workers, through their gangers, and the contractors, had always been a very personal one. Several firms succeeded in getting their own following to return to work, despite the immediate repudiation by Burns and the Central Strike Committee. These unilateral settlements did nothing to sustain Mr Norwood in the difficult position in which he had now been placed by the shipping companies on whom he should have been able to rely.

They had produced a policy calculated actively to embarrass the Joint Committee. They said : 'You are no longer able to discharge our ships or to dispose of their cargoes. It is obvious that your inept handling of labour has produced this strike, which will be the first of many. Why not allow us to do our own work ? We are quite certain that we can handle labour much better than you can.'

Mr Norwood rightly treated the demand as not only inopportune but impracticable. No doubt the shipping companies pictured a happy band of brothers advancing, all their demands gladly conceded, on the accumulated cargoes that congested the sheds. The Joint Committee, who owned the docks and understood the work done there, knew that so revolutionary a change in the daily working could be imposed only after a general settlement had led to normal working once more. The contentment foreseen by the shipping companies would need to be general. If Sir Donald Currie, speaking for the shipowners, had had his way, the Joint Committee's surrender to Burns could not have been long delayed. There were many within the docks' organisation that would have gladly jettisoned the ship discharge and loading and also the

Above Wapping entrance for shipping from the River Thames
to London Dock, 1856.
Below Seamen's Hospital Dispensary, Wall Street, London
Docks, 1881.

Above Weighing coir fibre in London Dock. The tally clerk can just be seen at the desk behind, 1930.
Below Wapping Basin, London Dock in 1931. This was the original entrance to the dock, built in 1805.

attendant quay work, but only 'when the present pressure is over, when we shall be quite ready to discuss the matter with our ship-owning customers', not all of whom, incidentally, supported Sir Donald Currie. Some had the good sense to see that a proprietary dock company, with its wide interests, could accomplish for a shipping company more than the latter, as an independent employer could do. They also saw the opportunities that a proliferation of employers—there were over 400 of these immediately prior to de-casualisation in 1967—would give the astute union official. From correspondence of the period I gleaned the following gem by a Joint Committee official, minuting on the proposed transfer of work : 'The men are ill-disciplined and a nuisance, the ship men with their independent ways are the cause of most of the trouble in the docks.'

Over the last half century, having got what they demanded, the shipping companies have been consistently unfortunate with their labour. During the same period the dock companies, and their successor the PLA, have kept their permanent men at work despite continued stoppages by other port labour. The PLA men were known in dockland as 'perms' and during a recent strike the wife of a pool labourer who was 'out' complained that a recent hair-do had come out. Her husband commented : 'Next time ask for a PLA perm, they never come out.'

After the change had been agreed it was wisely predicted by Sir Joseph Broodbank and others that peace in the docks would be unknown until labour had reverted to a single employer again. The truth of this has only been belatedly accepted. A condition of the 1967 decasualisation has been the reduction to a single figure of the number of port employers, with the port authority as do-minant. 'Re-organisation of the Ports'—the Government White Paper (January 1969) advocates the port authority as the single employer in each port. An article I wrote for the *Daily Telegraph* in June 1958, at a time when the work of the port of London had stopped because of a strike, and advocating a reduction in the number of port employers met with violent opposition. The or-ganisational changes that handed over the work in the lower docks to the shipowners (it was retained in the upper docks because of the tie-up with direct warehousing), overnight produced a mush-room growth of private employers. The irresponsible nature of many of these was to have a delaying effect on the many projects that the PLA was later to produce for the betterment of the docker and the expeditious handling of cargoes.

Whilst the argument on future work allocation was proceeding 'top-side' (the dockworkers' reference to City offices) Burns' ingenuity was kept busy in fund raising. The daily march was proving the most dependable means. Each day, to the slow music of the 'Dead March from Saul' the strikers, eight abreast, and led by two mounted policemen, took forty minutes to pass Dock House. They improved on this by a mammoth week-end march of 50,000 strikers and sympathisers from Tower Hill to Hyde Park. A large body of police was present to keep order but their services were not wanted. Neither were those of the Scots Guards held in readiness at Wellington Barracks, through the railings of which they were hailed as comrades by the strikers. The next day produced an even bigger procession, estimated at 60,000 men. Of these not even Burns could say which were genuine strikers. They turned out with fifteen bands and a flaunting of 200 banners. Many of these were aimed at the wicked landlord who was beginning to replace the employer as the villain of the piece. One banner had been painstakingly inscribed:

Our husbands are on strike, to the wives it is not honey
And we all think it right not to pay the landlord money
Everyone is on strike, so landlords do not be offended
The rent that's due we'll pay to you when the strike has ended.

Notices were already appearing in the windows of East End houses: 'As we are on strike landlords need not call.' On the pittance from the contributions of the public food came before rent.

Burns had the wisdom to welcome the many physical contributions that added to the number of the marchers and to the colour of the daily processions. The sharp outline of the dockers' struggle became blurred as the coal porters joined in, carrying on wheeled platforms, the ropes and baskets of their trade. The watermen paraded a real boat, and orange porters carried empty orange boxes on their shoulders. An international flavour was given to the daily procession when three American cattle ships contributed their combined crews of 150 sailors. The climax was reached on

38

Sunday, September 1st; the march had a truly catholic flavour. The Millwall Cornporters were present with their band, also a dozen branches of the Sons of the Phoenix Temperance, the Grand Order of Total Abstainers, and as a counterblast, the massed workers of the New Era Beer Company. A Mr Parrott entered the picture, self-appointed and conspicuous in a red blouse, 'mounted on a nondescript charger and acting in the capacity of a marshal'.

But whilst the weather remained fine and there was a certain amount of good clean fun on the fringe of the procession, the solid core of the strikers, their stomachs empty and their boots tied up with string, began to tire of the rigours of the daily march. By Burns' orders it was cancelled, only to be reinstated as soon as the immediate drop in contributions was evident.

And now a bitterness entered the struggle. At the preliminary Tower Hill meeting a striker was seen to mount the parapet 'bearing a lay figure enclosed in a long cloth'. A gory figure, recognisable as Mr Norwood, emerged from the winding sheets, together with a gallows whose purpose was only too clear. Armed with this sinister toy the daily procession now had a new attraction. With 'execrations of the most violent character aimed at Dock House, the grimy effigy was raised aloft, whilst the band thundered into the Marseillaise'. A later refinement substituted a coffin for the unwieldy gibbet. Containing the effigy of the unfortunate chairman the coffin was turned towards the windows whilst 'the large crowd appeared greatly to relish the huge joke'.

While these daily outings filled the collecting boxes, the docks were becoming hopelessly congested. It was a period of little unemployment; there was no general rush to take up the permanencies offered at £1 per week. The pickets were doing their job well. Meanwhile efforts were made by merchants and receivers of cargo to get their goods away from the docks. Top-hatted clerks from Mincing Lane offices, aided by the crews of strike-bound ships, trundled chests of tea over the cobblestones to vans that were prepared to defy the pickets. Staff of the New Zealand Shipping Company, helped by apprentices, managed to load sufficient cargo on their *Ruapehu* for her to sail. The employers' efforts to bring labour from other ports were thwarted by Burns' men who met these labourers at the London termini and gave them their fares home. In the early days of September not more than 500 blacklegs had taken advantage of the Directors' terms—£1 per week plus board and lodging within the docks, plus musical entertainments in the evenings.

Substantial efforts were made to bring about a settlement. The Lord Mayor, Sir James Whitehead, formed a committee of persons of importance and unimpeachable character to sit with him in his talks with the Directors. Included were Sir John Lubbock, Mr Sidney Buxton, a noted Liberal reformer and Cardinal Manning. At times representatives of the strike committee were brought in and City merchants offered their advice freely. At last, Mr Norwood, worn down by persistent argument, his own ill health and the defection of his allies, agreed to pay the dockers' tanner.

With their coffers empty the Joint Committee were not in a position to pay the extra penny until January 1st, 1890, by which time they hoped to have found the money by the imposition forthwith of higher dues and charges on ships and goods, these to be paid by the users of the port. The statement that the coffers were literally empty was confirmed by a colleague who, in 1925, told me that at the time of the strike, his father, a warehousekeeper at Tilbury Docks, had to wait the payment of his monthly salary until the shipping companies there had paid their bills. Having starved for five weeks the dockers now refused to wait a further ten weeks; ultimately the new rate was paid from November 4th, 1889.

On September 14th, 1889 the Central Strike Committee issued the laconic notice : 'End of strike—all men to return to work on Monday morning; by order of the Strike Committee.'

The public heaved a sigh of relief. To them, as with every strike since 1889, the return to work is assumed to be a return to normal conditions. Port authorities and shipping companies know only too well that escape from the daily headlines means that they are left alone to cope with the waiting ships and the accumulated cargoes that have piled up during the stoppage. Instead of the orderly return to work and—to use the modern jargon—the peaceful integration of the volunteer labour—Monday morning brought anarchy throughout the port. The complex nature of port work does not, and never will, permit the taking up of a myriad threads where they have been dropped some weeks ago. Each ship has to be assessed for the labour needed both in the holds and on the quay. Craft have to be in attendance and clerical staff at their posts. The railmen and the carmen have their part to play. The transportation machine had, during the five weeks of the stoppage, become so thoroughly jammed that not even with goodwill all round, could work have been found for more than a tithe of the clamouring applicants on the first morning.

Very little goodwill was available that Monday morning. Realising only that every new permanent man had taken, and would continue to take, the job of a man who had borne the burden and the heat of the last five weeks' strike, a savage onslaught was directed against the newcomers. No allowance was made for the impossibility of restarting the engine at full speed. Burns excused the brutal scenes of naked savagery and the fierce fighting that drove men, demented by fright, to escape over the Customs fence at the Royal Docks, only to be submerged in the filthy waters of the protective ditch that surrounded the dock perimeter. At other docks the few ex-strikers that were taken on walked out in disgust, demanding the instant dismissal of the volunteer element. At the South West India Docks, where the strike had started, the returning workers savagely attacked the volunteers, two of whom were put in hospital, and a further dozen injured, before the casual men were summarily paid off. The Cornporters at Millwall Docks publicly repudiated Burns and all his works, called for the immediate abolition of all foremen, marched off the ships and fought violently among themselves. As segregation of the blacklegs into gangs was by no means practicable and the casual men refused to work with them there was no resumption of work on Monday morning. Men who had starved for five weeks turned down employment that to them would have spelt affluence, in the certain knowledge that they had the power to chase the newcomers out of their jobs and out of the docks. This, after a few days of persistent terrorism, they succeeded in doing. Of the braver spirits who relied on the 'no victimisation, no discrimination' clause in the strike settlement, many fell victims to 'contrived' accidents, never difficult to bring about in dock working. Those who persisted in surviving were never assimilated into a labour force that despite its inherently casual nature, had discovered the power of a burning loyalty that it was never to lose. As late as 1921 men were pointed out to me at the West India Docks as having blacklegged in 1889.

What did the dock workers gain by a strike that has become

historic and the bitterness of which still lingers? Dockers have long memories and cannot forget the hot summer days of 1889.[1] Undoubtedly their own union organisation, which prior to the strike neither worker nor employer would have credited as being possible, was their greatest gain. It crystallised in an intense loyalty that sixty years later accepted without question, the order 'one out, all out'. In 1948, a period of intense stoppages, I was told by a union official of the T & GWU that anybody with a cap and a choker, on a bicycle, could ride round the West India Docks shouting 'they're all out at the Royals'. Men would come trooping off the ships with no questions asked and no regard to agreements or the current work. This attitude has been the most solid obstacle to reasoned argument ever since; agreements honourably made by union officials have been repudiated by the rank and file. All this was, however, trouble to come. The Directors had their hands full with immediate problems. For twelve months after the strike labour was unmanageable. It had tasted power and it was solidly organised in a new and comprehensive union, the Docks, Wharves and Riverside Workers' Union, of which Ben Tillet was the first General Secretary. Left out of this were the main specialist groups, the cornporters and the dealporters; they kept the identity of their own organisations until after the General Strike of 1926.

Consider what the unfortunate Directors had to contend with in the late autumn of 1889. Firstly, the Joint Committee which gave the London Company sixty-nine per cent of the annual profits, leaving only thirty-one per cent for the unfortunate shareholders of the East and West India Docks Company, saw little reason for initiative or enterprise. Having to absorb a bankrupt organisation the Joint Committee pursued a conservative policy, bothering only to retain existing business without making any attempt to secure new. The eleven years of its existence was a sterile time for the port of London and a penurious time for labour. Secondly, there was the imperative need to honour the promise to hand over to the shipping companies the right to do their own work and this involved the Directors in a complicated landlord-tenant relation that has regulated all ship and quay work in the lower docks and which exists today. Any intention that the Joint

[1] I saw a reference to the 1889 struggle in an issue of *The Port* for February 1969—eighty years after.

Committee might have had to improve or to decasualise labour was adjourned *sine die*, by the splintering of responsibility among the many employers that the new conditions introduced. As Sir Joseph Broodbank summed up the position : 'By allowing each shipowner to be a law unto himself as regards the conditions and terms of employment there was created a class of men receiving higher wages than the Joint Committee offered, but working irregularly, with heavy overtime pay one week and idleness the next, in busy times competed for by shipowners with surreptitious bonuses and in slack times left to fend for themselves.' The giving way to shipowners by the Joint Committee over this matter has been responsible, beyond any other single cause, for delaying general improvement in the conditions of dock labour.

As a consequence of the settlement there followed a reduction in the number of contractors. The Joint Committee had to accept the administrative burden of direct employment plus the cost of paying the men, always a deadhorse job, and this added to their costs. The settlement of 1889 had promised an extension of piecework, the working of which will be explained later. It also satisfied the men's desire for incentive working on a system that was not only fair but could be challenged at any time by the men concerned. The Joint Committee and their successors have always laboured under a severe disadvantage in that they were, at the top, scrupulously honest in their dealings with labour; their records are open to inspection by the men's representatives and their officials lean over backwards to honour agreements. True as this is— and it is a remarkably fine record and one conceded by both unions —it makes no provision for, nor does it tolerate 'under the counter' payments. Every man is entitled to his pound of flesh as laid down in the national agreements, neither more nor less. Human nature being what it is, and never more so than in dockland, the PLA have always been handicapped in attracting labour, against some of the less scrupulous stevedores.

From this period sprang the system of 'Contingency Allowance' which has since been a minor field of disputes. In taking over the work hitherto done by the contractors, the Joint Committee were faced with demands made by individuals for payment in recognition of superior skill. In a gang measuring and piling hardwood one man measured the length of each piece; another man acted as

43

the front piler and was responsible for the symmetry and the safety of the pile. The principle was acceded that, in the contingency of men being able to exercise these and other skills, a payment of a few coppers per working period would be made. These have become known as 'Cons' and they soon built up into a formidable list. Some are now out of date, but the list is a monument to the principle that where all men are equal some are entitled to be more equal than others. In fairness it must be conceded that the 'Con' system provides a simple machine for rewarding and encouraging the new dock skills such as mobile crane and forklift truck driving that have now replaced many of the early craft payments.

With the Chairman a dying man, with labour that was largely unmanageable and was already learning to spread the work by working to rule, riven from within by opposing claims of the two rival companies and reviled from without for giving away too much and acting too late, the Joint Committee was in no mood to consider any amelioration of the casual conditions that were substantially resumed after the strike was over. Times were unpropitious, trade remained stationary for the next decade and there was no call for improvement in cargo handling. It was a static period and labour, having gained their 6d. an hour and a recognised half-hour for their dinner, remained in a sullen mood, concentrating on minor exploitations of the new piecework system and the 'Con' payments.

I have spent time and space on a description of the Great Strike because, in the history of the London portworker, no event of similar importance has occurred. Also from the Press of the period and from official papers that I have been able to peruse, it is possible to build up a detailed background to the daily life of the casual worker in the late nineteenth century.

6

After the dust raised in 1889 had settled, social reformers and critics of the Joint Committee observed that the multiplication of employers that followed the decision of the Committee to jettison their discharging work in the lower dock had produced a half-hundred margins of unemployed labour where before there had been only one on each department. Every little employer now had his own place of call; every call place produced its own quota of discontented labourers who had backed the wrong horse. The remedy advocated to the Directors was to decasualise labour. The Directors knew that by splintering the employing market they had postponed indefinitely any workable port scheme of this kind. They knew only too well that their financial position did not, nor was it ever likely to, permit their paying full wages to men for whom no work could be found. It was inherent in the dock business that this should be so.

It is greatly to their credit, as the major port employer, that in the early 1890s the Joint Committee did produce a sound and workable scheme for improving the conditions of dockers. It ensured labour peace until 1911; it was adopted by the PLA in 1909. Until the Second War brought into being the National Dock Labour Board it regulated the employers' relations with the port-workers.

Firstly there was the staff of permanent men. This varied in the number as business thrived or was depressed. Apart from guaranteed employment the permanent men enjoyed a paid holiday, sick pay, and after fifteen years' service could claim a benevolent allowance to a maximum of ten shillings a week if overtaken by sickness or old age. In the days before Lloyd George's Old Age

Pension at seventy (1911) of five shillings a week, this was a considerable benefit. As things settled down after the 1889 strike, the permanent men employed by the Joint Committtee were recognised as the élite of the East End, a position held by their descendants until 1967.

Next in importance were the men on the 'A' List, from which recruitment to the permanent staff was made. These men were guaranteed a week's work at a time; they also enjoyed the paid holidays.

Working downwards we come to the 'B' men who were casuals employed as required. Their status consisted of being attached to a 'home' department, on whose 'B' List they could work their way to the top. They were taken on for work by numbers and every quarter the departmental 'B' List was revised in the light of the attendances put in and the individual skill and conduct of the men. On the whole, and I speak from experience, the 'B' men, if their affairs were properly managed, formed a valuable and reliable source of skilled labour. In some meat departments where work took place on certain week-days only, the labour was drawn entirely from the 'B' men. Vacancies on the 'A' List were filled by 'B' men who had impressed the departmental officers.

Below this level were the out-and-out casuals, dimly recognised as 'C' men. They held no status save what they could make for themselves by devotion to duty on the few occasions when they could catch the eye of the taking-on foreman. By dint of 'following' assiduously a particular department and by some luck in securing enough work to leave an impression, 'C' men were able to take their place at the foot of the 'B' List. They were also useful for jobs of a domestic kind that by their regularity and absence of piecework earnings did nothing to attract 'B' men. In 1921 when I took over the now defunct West Wood Wharf at the West India Docks, I inherited, to my satisfaction, two C men who kept the department, mainly open timber sheds with earthen floors, scrupulously clean. Both were probably in their seventies but they needed no supervision. It was with genuine regret that I had, during the Geddes economies of the 1920s, to put these two excellent workers off.

A 'B' man enjoyed an extra-territorial status. Sensing that his home department would be slack on the morrow he would present himself at a busy department (in his own or even in a 'foreign' dock) where he could claim employment after all the home department's 'B' men had been taken on. To help him in getting work it became the custom to post each night at the dock gates a forecast of the extra labour required the following morning at each department. In addition to this official intimation the 'B' men had their own very efficient grapevine. It told them where they could best try out their luck for the next day or even for an unexpected midday call. During the years of the Depression the 'B' men had to keep their ears to the ground if they were to survive. How else explain the occasions, and they were several, when, during the morning, I would tell the foreman that we should need another gang at 1 p.m. and at 12.45 there would be several hundred men fighting for the thirteen jobs on offer?

Although the Joint Committee had given up control of the large labour forces at the lower docks, the more responsible of the private employers did introduce parallel schemes but tailored to their own requirements. From these developed the 'choice' gangs that could depend on fairly regular employment. Men began to specialise on jobs such as sugar discharge. The premier master stevedore in London prior to 1939 had trained his choice gangs to discharge 500 tons of Cuban sugar (in three-hundredweight bags) in eight hours, no mean feat and one that ensured that he and his men were seldom out of work, albeit too old at forty.

Portworkers are notorious for their contrariness. I worked hard as Traffic Superintendent, during the early years after the Second War, to bring the Authority's depleted list of permanent men to an acceptable number. It had fallen from some 3,000 in 1939 to 1,649 in 1948 when authority was at last given for further recruitment. Overjoyed, I told the Dock Superintendents to go ahead and to build up their strength to the numbers they had sought. A week later I was told that the recruiting was going badly. Many 'B' men likely to make reliable permanent workers had been interviewed but few had jumped at the chance of a regular job. Pressed for their reasons for refusing what we, in our ignorance of the docker, had fought the management to secure for him, it was explained that they had no objection to work as such but enough was enough. In the boom conditions that then prevailed a good worker could pick his own job. When one job came to an end he might take two or three days off, or wait until he could snare another well-paid job at the same, or at another, department. There was a strong feeling, it was still there at the time of decasualisation in 1967, that a permanent man soon became the slave of the management. The unfettered casual could come and go as he pleased and he was loth, not seeing the shape of things to come, to give this up. There was something in the argument that the cautious PLA permanent labourer never came out on strike whereas the casual was ready at the magic cry of 'One out, all out' to drop his hook, break any agreement that his union had made and throw his cap over the nearest windmill. This jocund outlook did the port much harm; today the container has cast its shadow over the sunny work outlook which the casual man of the 1950s developed.

And so the 1890s saw some amelioration in the harsh working conditions. Trade improved and the standard of living was moving upwards. The old century closed and the new one began in a blaze of prosperity and imperial satisfaction. One considerable cause of this, to the docker who could see a few years ahead, was the disappearance of the ill-fated Joint Committee. The unhappy arrangement by which the East and West India Docks Company had been put in the position of inferiority for eleven years came to an end on January 1st, 1901 with the formation of the London and India Docks Company. The Surrey Commercial and the Millwall Docks Companies, the first prosperous and the second teetering on the verge of bankruptcy, were still independent enterprises, although their arrangements for labour were similar to those of the larger docks. To many who were farsighted enough to see the lines on which the major port of the United Kingdom must develop, the new company had been formed to preside over its own obsequies. The traffic flowing into and out of London and increasing each year, was hampered not only by the out-of-date conditions within the docks but by the lack of dredging of the river, essential to maintain a deep water channel to the dock entrances. In the very year of its inception the Company had to face a Royal Commission appointed 'to enquire into the present administration of the port' and 'to report whether any change or improvement is necessary'. Mr Cator Scott, the first Chairman of the London and India Docks Company, made an impressive showing before the Commission but a government Bill was introduced in 1903 proposing that the recently formed London County Council should run the port. With the confidence that was born of complete ignorance of the subject, the LCC offered to take over the docks and the river as a department of their enterprise. However, the Corporation of the City of London would not be dispossessed of their very ancient rights over riparian properties, the wharfingers showed no enthusiasm for the change and the government quietly dropped the bill at the end of the 1904 session.

This put back the inevitable a few years. At the opening of Tilbury Docks in 1886 Sir Donald Currie, a name to conjure with in the shipping world, had pointed out the futility of competition which, whilst it benefited shipowners, could only deprive the dock proprietors of the means by which they could provide the facilities for which port users were clamouring. The docks of Liverpool had, in the mid-century, been placed under a Harbour Board, but many years of fruitless competition, in which labour was a substantial sufferer, were to ensue before unified control came to London. The Liberal Government that swept into power at the end of 1905 paid early attention to the condition of the Thames and its docks. The driving force at the Board of Trade was Mr Lloyd George. He piloted the Port of London Bill through Parliament and the ensuing Act became operative on April 1st, 1909, under his successor, Mr Winston Churchill. After setting out the constitution of the new authority and, greatly daring for the times, two members representing organised labour were included, it was enacted that the conditions enjoyed by labour under the separate dock companies would continue. The Millwall Docks Company welcomed the take-over; the Surrey Commercial Docks Company dispersed the liquid assets of their Board Room to the Directors and at the last Board Meeting they solemnly stood to attention as the Company flag was raised to half-mast. The London and India Docks Company staff naturally took most of the plums that the new organisation provided.

Shipowners, wharfingers and the smaller employers in the port could now look to the single authority for a lead. They did not look in vain. Mr Hudson Ewbank Kearley, Parliamentary Secretary to the Board of Trade, and later the first Viscount Devonport, was the first Chairman. A self-made merchant, he was a man of strong character who had no time for appeasement or vacillation. As an instance of his methods, the PLA in 1917 were forced to

49

increase their port charges. The Board of Trade objected and refused permission. Lord Devonport called a special meeting of the Authority, obtained the signatures of all the members to a joint resignation, and took this personally to the Board of Trade. He placed this on the desk of the President and said : 'Now you can run the PLA yourself.' Needless to say, Mr Walter Long gave in without a struggle and the matter is now recorded in the Authority's Minutes of the period.

Under his autocratic rule, which lasted until 1925, the port of London prospered. His first master plan included the dredging of the River Thames and the development of the docks. The major project was the building of the King George V Dock, opened in 1921, on ground that had been bought by the India Docks Company, south of their Royal Albert Dock at Silvertown. No longer did the trumpet give an uncertain note. There were many who doubted that a corporative body could successfully run a major port. They would have preferred a municipal body such as Bristol enjoyed. The independent main line railways ran their own ports. Southampton and Hull were the principal ones and many thought these were successful. In the long run and with the benefit of hindsight, it can be said that the new authority did the job that they were given to do—members were unpaid—in a prompt and efficient manner. The Board included shipowners, merchants, wharfingers, master lightermen, master stevedores and officers appointed by the Admiralty and Trinity House. With the English genius for compromise, these interests, which privately tried either to compete with or exploit the docks, combined to make the port of London in those days, the greatest port in the world. This happy result I can, speaking from experience, attribute to the force and the driving power that originated with the Chairman, and which was felt throughout his command. Efficiency was the watchword. Mr Gradgrind was still a power in the City and the man who failed expected, and got, little mercy from those above him.

Into the camp of labour came an awareness that the happy days when one employer could be played against another had gone. Following discussions among the many unions that claimed to represent dockers' interests, the National Transport Workers' Federation was formed in 1910. The first President was Mr Harry Gosling, secretary to the Amalgamated Society of Watermen and

Lightermen. He subsequently became one of the two labour members of the Board of the PLA. I last saw him in the hall of the Head Office in Leadenhall Street, having just finished the excellent lunch that preceded the opening ceremony by H.M. King George V of the new dock to which he gave his name. Gosling was wearing a straw hat, it was July in 1921, a large rose was in his buttonhole and he was smoking an outsize cigar—the perfect picture of a contented capitalist.

7

Gosling made an application in 1911 to Lord Devonport for a number of concessions to dock labour. In the early stages, according to Sir Joseph Broodbank, the Chairman of the Authority's Dock and Warehouse Committee and the Chairman's technical adviser, all was sweetness and light. No one paid higher compliments to the accessibility and the reasonableness of the employers' Chairman than did Harry Gosling. Lord Devonport had brought into the negotiations the great shipping companies and also the wharfingers; this time there was not going to be any shooting from the rear, as in the days of poor Mr Norwood. Gosling compared London most favourably with other port authorities with whom he had negotiated. In this pleasant atmosphere the Devonport Agreement was born. It was a period when the public conscience was disturbed about conditions in the sweated industries, the match girls, the chainmakers and the needleworkers of Redditch. There was much goodwill towards the dockers; much of this came from the port employers. The new agreement gave the men 7d. an hour with corresponding overtime rates. Work was to begin at 7 a.m. instead of 6 a.m. as hitherto and a full hour (unpaid) was granted for dinner, thus enabling many of the men to eat a good meal in their own homes. Minimum employment for four hours was conceded; previously men could be taken on for as little as half an hour for a payment of 3d. Double pay was promised to men working on Sundays or Bank Holidays. Everywhere the Devonport Agreement was hailed as a new dawn in the dock labour world. The bad old days were at last over and dockwork would no longer be classed as a depressed industry. It remained only for the formal agreement of the rank and file of the Federation to be added and a Mass Meeting was called immediately.

What happened at this meeting will never be known now. Two days later Gosling ordered all his members to cease work. The Devonport Agreement was repudiated. To provide some colour for their action the men fabricated a demand for another penny an hour. Lord Devonport was not a man to be intimidated, although he was genuinely nonplussed at finding that the word of a union leader was not his bond. That the agreement made by a labour leader can be so much waste paper, a fact that is accepted with little comment today, was something new in 1911. Practical men of that time explained Gosling's want of ordinary honesty by the suggestion that the generous and courteous treatment he had received from Lord Devonport, a man at all times able to carry out to the letter what he had promised, had given Gosling a power complex for which there was no foundation. Gosling was no Ernest Bevin, for whom the dockers had to wait another decade. When he saw those with whom he had negotiated put their signatures to the Devonport Agreement he no doubt thought that his signature would carry the same weight. The first labour man to be treated by the employers as an equal, he did not realise that he had automatically become 'one of them' overnight, in the eyes of his members. When he appeared at the meeting he was immediately cut down to size. He should have had the honesty to resign his position. That he did not take this simple step did irreparable harm to the public image of the union leader; relations between the two sides deteriorated to those of 1889. All the excellent work put in during the previous twenty-two years went for nought as the long hot days of the summer of 1911 saw the dust settle once again on the docks of London. Some 1,500 of the PLA permanent men left their work; the casual men responded en masse.

Those who saw the pattern of 1889 as emerging again misjudged Lord Devonport. Where Mr Norwood had been embarrassed by the tepid support, at the best, of the shipowners and the wharfingers, Lord Devonport insisted that their interests were, in this matter, identical with the Authority. The defection of any port employer would not be tolerated. Neither had he any use for Mansion House Committees or eminent dignatories of the Church.

The work, he pointed out to Mr Lloyd George who saw himself in the role of peacemaker, was still at the docks waiting to be done. The agreement that bore his name set out the terms on which it would be done. Any man who wanted work could have it. As for the men's leaders, they had by their conduct ceased to exist as far as he was concerned; he did not propose to have any further dealings with them. Lord Devonport, like all great leaders, saw complex problems very clearly. Not even the most optimistic of labour leaders could find a ray of hope in this attitude. John Burns, now gainfully employed as President of the Local Government Board in Asquith's Cabinet, was wise enough not to interfere. Lacking even this support, the strike was called off on August 11th. The next move was now with the unions who set about looking for an excuse. It had always been a custom of the port that employers should call their casual labour inside the dock. An attempt after the 1889 strike to have union representatives present at these calls, in order to check that the men held union cards, had been defeated. To salve something from the humiliating defeat of 1911, labour sought, and was given by a few employers only, a concession. The casual men they took on should be called at places immediately outside the dock gates. The union officials were thus able to move among the men to check union cards and, at times, to address the waiting men from a soap box.

This argument of when and where the men should be called started in 1889. It has only been resolved by the decasualisation of 1967. No effort aimed at speeding up the work, no granting of amenities inside the dock nor any form of relief offered by the employers has prevailed over the men's undoubted right to be their own masters until they physically enter the portals of the dock. It may be, and very often is, raining outside; inside is warmth and some comfort. Calling-on buildings have been put up, all to little purpose. I have already quoted Lord Devlin in his recent report on the docker's refusal to accept change even when it is for his own good. As a young man I often had to supervise the recommencement of work after the supper interval. This was timed for 11 p.m. The Authority's men would report at that time, all present and correct. At 11.15 and not before, the stevedores who were loading the ship moved, although I could never spot the signal, from the place where they had been standing since before eleven o'clock, the few yards into the dock. My foreman, a veteran of the department, could give no explanation. 'They're just bloody minded. They think they are maintaining a right, what it is neither they nor anyone else knows,' and he shrugged his shoulders at the ineffable stupidity of his fellow workers.

Out of this minor concession the Federation now proceeded to build up a strong case. Firstly they represented the stoppage of 1911 as a success. They claimed that by it the men had achieved the beneficial working conditions of the Devonport Agreement. That it had been signed and was therefore effective two days before the strike was engineered, a few of the workers knew. Secondly, if the Federation could win its fight for a closed shop then indeed could it demand recognition as a national body with the right to negotiate for all the major ports. If the employers could be cajoled into supporting the closed shop by the growing power of a national union, then Lord Devonport, as also the leading lights in all the other ports, would find themselves acting as recruiting agents for the union.

Since 1912 we have seen many nations that were keyed up ready for a war and who have found little difficulty in producing a cause. On May 19th, 1912 certain of the lightermen refused to acknowledge a fellow worker who, they claimed, was not a member of the union. Immediately and without formulating any demands, other transport workers downed tools. No grievances were expressed. The notice to cease work that should have been given was ignored. The port came to a standstill. The Liberal Government under Asquith set a precedent without which none of its many successors could have stayed the course. An Official Enquiry was appointed to ascertain the details of the dispute. Once and for all it was established that 'An Enquiry a day keeps action away'.

Lord Devonport took the line that could with advantage have been taken by his successors, right up to decasualisation. He ignored the Enquiry completely as the waste of time that he, and the government, knew it to be—as also have most of its successors. The Federation demanded a closed shop throughout the ports. This would be brought about by pressure from the port authorities on the smaller employers, until every docker was safely in the union fold. Employers would be expected to refuse work to non-unionists and they would also satisfy themselves in the case of their tendering exports to stevedores loading a ship, that all the latter were members of the Federation. Naturally Lord Devonport and his fellow employers would have none of this poppycock. That it never succeeded I knew by the fact that in the 1930s certain dockers were pointed out to me as non-unionists.

How did the Federation, so soon after its defeat, succeed in calling out the majority of the dockworkers and why, with no funds for strike pay, did the latter so readily respond to the unaccustomed union whip? The answer lay in the intensive organisation that the Federation had put in during the winter of 1911–12. A body of paid delegates had been at work for some months with satisfactory results. Versed in union rules, skilled in argument and with nothing to lose, they burrowed their way into the working lives of the members. With the complicated piecework structure that existed no delegate looking for a grievance had far to seek. They were well able to stand up to the local officers, both of the Authority and the shipping companies, and often to best them in argument. Very quickly the men came to rely on their local delegates who did the work of the shop steward and, since decasualisation, have been so called.

The crude technique of intimidation used in earlier strikes had improved greatly. The brute bludgeoning of 1889 had not been entirely successful. Blacklegs were elusive and many were, like some animals, dangerous; when attacked they had defended themselves. With a lack of chivalry that has unfortunately been a continuous feature of dock disputes, intimidation was now switched to the wife and family of the non-unionist. It was not sufficient that at his work the non-unionist was sent to Coventry by his mates and suffered more accidents than the Federation member. When he reached home he found 'SCAB' chalked on his front door, panes of glass broken, his wife in tears and his children with tales of maltreatment at school. It was not a pretty picture. Union officials have deplored the practice whilst assiduously ensuring that it was kept alive. It is not very easy for people living in country or suburban neighbourhoods to realise the effect that this treatment had on working class families living cheek by jowl in the crowded East End. The butcher refusing to give the usual credit, the neighbour refusing to take in groceries or to keep an eye on the children—all the little acts of goodwill that are taken for granted and which become more important with a lower standard of living, all were withdrawn. Insults, and an occasional brickbat from unidentified youngsters, to his family wore down a man's resistance quickly. Living as they did, they had no escape from the daily persecution.

'Peaceful persuasion' was how the Union justified this despicable practice. The material advancement of the docker was their main object. If the non-unionist, his wife and his kids got hurt because he elected not to help in this, then such trifles as personal principles or individual justice could not be allowed to interfere. It was a dreadful weapon for the union to adopt as the standard practice it has since become. The worker was hit in his most vulnerable places. The police were not interested because official complaint was not made. No Home Secretary has deigned to take notice of a practice so alien to his own comfortable way of life.

However, conditions were different from 1889. There was no John Burns to lead a daily procession. Traffic had so increased that so picturesque a means of getting money could not now be considered. The issue, to the man in the street and largely to the docker, was academic. Newspapers can understand the picture of a starving docker asking for another penny an hour and in 1889 had put over the story to the public. They were not, in 1912, interested in a struggle for the aggrandisement of the Federation. In their hearts many who would have supported the strike were disgusted at the un-English coercion of the non-unionist and his family. There was also a considerable number of unemployed; within two weeks of the commencement of the stoppage 8,000 men were at work in the docks. Although the strike had been sparked by the lightermen they do not seem, as a class, to have been enthusiastic about its continuance. By the efforts of the master lightermen and their staff sufficient craft were back in work to make the dock situation fluid. This hundred per cent refusal to handle craft had made the work of the 1889 volunteers largely ineffective. It was remarked at the time that the master lightermen had successfully continued to rule the waves by waiving most of the rules. In 1912 the government had grasped the fact that a complete stoppage in the port of London could quickly affect the cost of living. Police protection was given to lorries, mostly horse drawn, laden with food, as they left the docks. Fourteen years later, when these had been largely replaced with petrol and steam-driven lorries I saw from the Clock Tower of the East India Dock, during the General Strike, a convoy moving slowly from the Royal Docks, escorted by armoured cars and light tanks.

Seeing that the strike was going sour on them the union leaders dropped the closed shop issue. 'That cock won't fight' was the conclusion to which they were forced to come. Hasty demands for higher pay and shorter hours were put to the, by now, uninterested, employers. The final blunder was a demand for uniform pay for all dock workers. It was a blunder because the union should certainly have known that the pay structure of dockers is traditionally riddled with inequalities, anomalies and anachronisms. I have already mentioned the system of 'Cons'—payment of a few coppers for special skill. In an industry where, in theory at least although never in practice, all were equal, it was essential that some should be more equal than the rest. The few coppers daily that the winch driver drew had an immense status value. It meant that someone was getting less pay than he was and this, whatever the rank, is a pleasant feeling.

The last weapon in the Federation's hands was personal invective. Not the coffin paraded outside Dock House windows; ideas of humour were more sophisticated since the rough and tumble of 1889. Ben Tillet however still had a sense of the macabre and he still had the ear of the strikers at their daily mass meeting on Tower Hill. After the daily ration of pie-in-the-sky a helping of caviare followed. He invited his huge audience, and this included many of the public, to accompany him to the Throne of Grace, there to place before the Almighty a simple request. It was one which, if granted, could usher in the millennium where all dockers' strikes would be successful. Whilst his grubby audience bowed their bared heads, Ben Tillet gazed towards the heavens, declaiming in a loud voice :

'Oh God, strike Lord Devonport dead.'

It is a matter of history that this unusual invocation failed. Lord Devonport lived for another twenty-two years to invite Ben Tillet to spend week-ends at his house at Marlow. Many of the staff from the London Docks, as well as from the Head Office, attended this daily ritual, before scurrying back to see if the result had been spectacular enough to justify cutting down their lunch hour.

A half-hearted appeal to Lloyd George, Lord Haldane and John

Burns came to nothing. Asquith advised Gosling to throw in the sponge. On July 29th, 1912, after a stoppage of ten weeks, the men presented themselves for work. There was no repetition of the scenes that marred the resumption of work in 1889. The strike had lasted so long that many men had left the industry, many more had quietly drifted back. The boot this time was very much on the other foot. Lord Devonport refused to reinstate any permanent labourers. They were allowed to apply individually for a position on the 'B' list of their former department. After work had been found for all the permanent men, including those made permanent during the strike, the 'B' men would be taken on in numerical order. Such was the inglorious end to the third of the major officially led strikes. The strike of 1912 caused much bad blood, putting the cause of decasualisation back for many years.

8

The First War held no such immediate threat to normal civil life as did the Second War, twenty-five years later. Rather was there the tendency to leave the war to Kitchener's Army and the professionals whose hands were full, equipping and training the thousands of volunteers. In any case the war would, it was certain, be over by Christmas 1914. The slogan 'Business as Usual' was invented. The submarine menace took two years before it began to affect the trade of our ports. At no time was the French coast in enemy hands. Apart from the loss of Reservists among labour, employers in London were able to carry on much as usual.

The PLA did not let their recent setbacks of 1911 and 1912 interfere with plans to improve the status of the dockers who now included the newcomers from the 1912 settlement. If they were never welcomed they were at least tolerated. In October 1914 plans matured before the outbreak of war were introduced. A big step towards decasualisation was made with the establishment of permanent men fixed at 3,000, later increased to 4,000. That figure today seems high but it indicated the large number of men needed to handle the infinite quantity of packages that together made up the cargo of a general ship some fifty years ago. Literally each package was handled individually. In 1968 one read of the maiden voyage of a 940 container ship—that is, 940 lifts are required to discharge a fully laden ship, three times the size of those in 1914. The hand truck with its few variants, was the only means of transporting goods from the quay to the shed and vice versa. The electric truck that carried a load of a ton or over did not arrive until the early 1920s and for years it had very limited use. The basic wage had been fixed at 7d. an hour by the Devonport Agreement, or 28s. a week for a working week of six days. The long-standing grievance that the basic wage remained unaltered throughout a man's service was now remedied by the granting of an increment of one shilling weekly after two years' satisfactory service as a permanent labourer. With a further similar increment to be earned after four years, the docker could take home 30s. for six days' work, *irrespective of overtime or piecework earnings, both available to the steady permanent docker.* Six days' paid annual leave, a considerable concession when Fourth Class Clerks enjoyed only ten days, were also granted. At the pleasure of the Authority there was also the maximum benevolent allowance of 10s. a week after the age of seventy. There was no sick pay. Under Lloyd George's much reviled insurance scheme—ninepence for fourpence as the gibe went—the State accepted liability for relief during sickness and absence due to accidents.

Piecework, which had originally been extorted from the employers by men certain that they could earn more than their elderly and less capable colleagues, had now become a general feature of dockwork. Still regarding it with suspicion and cutting and chopping pennies per ton off well-paying rates, the Authority used the system as a means of maintaining the principle of the mobility of labour. Permanent men agreed to being transferred from their home department as work offered at another department or at another dock. An efficient system of advising labour requirements overnight was instituted and ship men not wanted in London Docks reported to the West India Docks the following morning. Some transfers were even made during the dinner hour. The dockers were thus able to their advantage to move from one piecework job to another. Ship men came in for the maximum overtime. There were some defects in the system.

When work could not be found at other departments there was perforce a general downgrading. Men who drove winches or cranes took their places in the gangs or were relegated to quay or even to warehouse work. In the last resort domestic duties, sweeping floors and cleaning warehouse windows, work that was paid on the basic rate, was all that was left to the permanent men. Men who could not, by reason of age or disability, hold their own in the piecework, and the pace became increasingly arduous as rates continued to be cut, found a useful niche in jobs such as mending bags or cases, looking after the transit sheds or even ministering to the personal needs of senior dock officers. Many a good meal—a haddock that cost 3*d.*—has been cooked for me and my fellow officers on overtime work, by a labourer whose piecework days were over.

This very major attack on the casual system did much to rationalise the ever-varying demands for labour. With every dock department having its own following of casual men and with every following producing its daily surplus of unwanted labour, the total throughout the docks area was still cruelly high. With a floating staff of 4,000 men opportunities for casual men became less. Knowing that vacancies would be filled from other docks the casual, with no claims for employment, looked for other work. His chances were further diminished by a reorganisation of Preference dock labour. The 'A' list was abolished. Each department was granted its own establishment of 'B' men, taken on for work strictly by priority of individual members. Each quarter the 'B' list of each department was revised; men who had attended well and shown aptitude were 'promoted' higher up the list. This made a very real difference to their daily chance of work, as well as their ultimate selection for a permanency. Attendance of casual men was further discouraged by the right accorded to 'B' men to be taken on at other than their home department, prior to work being offered to casuals.

Unfortunately the 'specialists', the cornporters and the dealporters with their peculiar traditions and working conditions, were not amenable to absorption in the general labour of the port. The specialist nature of their duties was thus perpetuated; they remained a potential source of friction for another half a century. I remember that, in 1938, in view of the shortage of work for cornporters the PLA agreed with the T & GWU to grant these men 'B' tickets on a busy ship discharging department. After a trial period of six months the concession was withdrawn because only a minute number of attendances had been made. The thirty or so 'B' tickets could, and would, have been more usefully enjoyed by non-specialist applicants of whom there were many. It does show how difficult it can be for men of goodwill to help the docker.

The scheme had been born into a world that was soon to be riven by the greatest war through which London had lived. Nevertheless it was a success. It remained the basic system on which the National Dock Labour Scheme was constructed by Ernest Bevin, the Wartime Minister of Labour, in 1941. One of its best features, of which I still retain the most pleasant recollections, was the personal relations that grew between the London employer, his staff of permanent men and his following of 'B' men. Every dock officer knew each of these personally. We knew—it was an essential part of our job—the capabilities of each man, those who could and would take responsibility as gangers or crane drivers and on whom one could rely to do a difficult job. We knew also the man 'who would spoil a good job and make a bad job worse', in the language of his mates. This happy relation was enjoyed by all master stevedores and practical dock officers.

By 1915 about 7,000 men were daily finding work in the port of London. By March 1918, owing to the rate of sinkings and the diversion of American warlike stores to the French ports, tonnage entering London had fallen to seventy per cent of pre-war figures. The part that the docker had played in the war effort found practical recognition in his exemption from the Conscription Acts. A move to fit round pegs into round holes was made with the formation of the first Transport Workers Battalions, the 16th York and Lancaster Regiment. Originally intended for use in home ports, these dockers in khaki were the forerunners of the Port Operating Groups (originally the Docks Groups) of the Royal Engineers, to whose distinguished role in the Second War it will be a privilege later to refer. Wherever the supply of civil port labour was insufficient the Transport Battalions were sent. Faced in 1916 with the chaotic conditions in the French ports, Sir Eric Geddes, the Director General of Transportation in the B.E.F., called for their services overseas. By the end of 1918, 15,000 dockers were in uniform. The system combined the merits of discipline in working, speed in action and economy in cost.

In February 1915 a new term appeared in dockland. The advancing cost of living, which the government was unable to stop, was met by a War Bonus. Three shillings a week were added to the dockers' basic pay. By the end of the war this had been advanced, by stages, to thirty-two shillings.

With higher wages came a demand for a shorter working week to be brought about by work in the docks ceasing at twelve noon on Saturdays. To a generation that looks askance at work of any kind, for themselves, on Saturday, the revolutionary nature of this demand will not be appreciated. My first day's work as a junior clerk in London Docks had been a Saturday. During the morning I was casually told that work went on until four o'clock, as on other days. However, the demand for the same overall payment for less working hours was conceded in April 1919. Essential work on ship turnround continued; after twelve noon it was paid on overtime rates. This was the first of many moves for a shorter basic week in the full knowledge that the same number of hours would be worked, but several of them would be more highly paid. After the Second War one such demand was pressed on account of the cultural needs of the docker.

An immediate shipping boom followed the Armistice of 1918. Once more the seas were free of the menace that had confined sailings to convoys. London, as with other ports, quickly became congested. The original government scheme provided for the immediate demobilisation of men essential to the restoration of industry. This had quickly given way to one that appealed more to the nation's sense of fairness—'First in, first out'. By the middle of 1919 the docks were alive with young and hardy men from the three services. Faced with congestion on every side the Authority took on more permanent men. It could be said that this period produced the major attempt at decasualisation, prior to the national movement that culminated in September 1967. This force of permanent men was largely formed from ex-service men who had had their fill of discipline. Work was plentiful all over the country. The Federation was in the mood for a demand that would end all demands.

It came in October 1919. The working week was to remain at forty-four hours, with a basic wage of two shillings an hour; normal overtime was to be paid at three shillings an hour. The demand was a national one.

John Burns had lost his seat at Battersea at the Coupon General Election in December 1918. He must have smiled wryly as he thought back thirty years to the struggle for the Dockers' Tanner.

No national body of employers existed, with whom a national agreement could be negotiated. The few major ports employed the bulk of dock labour but in the long run eighty-one ports were

64

parties to the subsequent agreement. Once more Lord Devonport took the lead for he saw clearly that the Federation must be recognised and that any attempt to negotiate on a port, or even on a regional basis, would lead to the employers being hopelessly out-pointed.

And so the stage was set. On February 3rd, 1920, the Court of Enquiry appointed by the Minister of Labour, under the presidency of Lord Shaw of Dunfermline, had their first meeting. He was aided by eight members, representing both sides. The employers' case was in the hands of Sir Lynden Macassey, an ornament of the English Bar. The men's case was put by Ernest Bevin, an ex-milkman from Bristol. His unorthodox but very pertinent presentation of his case quickly gained the headlines; overnight he became 'the dockers' K.C.'. His opponent, a legal luminary of the correct candle power, was speedily eclipsed. The President took little trouble to disguise his sympathy with the dockers.

Bevin's brief included no haggling over halfpennies. He demanded that the dockers be recognised as human beings, entitled to good and ample food. When the men, in the nature of the industry, were not required to work, they should be maintained by the employers, against the time when they were next wanted. Bevin in 1920 as the Federation Secretary had not the power to bring about so great a change. Bevin as Minister of Labour in 1941 introduced the National Dock Labour Board, which was brought into existence to implement this same principle. He also argued for the setting up of a conciliation scheme that would give the men's representatives a voice in the daily working of the port, particularly on the piecework side. Bevin's whole argument fitted perfectly into the background of Lloyd George's 'Land fit for Heroes'. Many of the dockers for whom he spoke were the heroes that the country had in mind. His tour-de-force came when he brought into court stinted portions of the more stable foods that he claimed were all that a married docker with three children could buy on his earnings. This was front-page news, for the Press compared the dockers' mite with the sumptuous fare enjoyed on the wartime profits of the shipowners and which were publicly known to have been immense. I remember the front page of the *Evening Standard* with its photographs of Bevin's evidence, alongside the typical shipowners' (imagined) dinner.

For the dockers it was a case of 'all this and Bevin too'. In spite of a minority report signed by Sir Joseph Broodbank and Mr Frederick Scrutton, a leading master stevedore, the agreement of May 5th, 1920 embodied his main demands.

During a period of comparative leisure brought about by one of the many strikes of the post-1945 era, I took the trouble to read through the verbatim report of the Shaw Award, as it became known. On the one hand there was the brave show made by Bevin; on the other the rather divided show that the employers made. During Lord Devonport's evidence he was asked his opinion on a working matter at the port of Sharpness. Without hesitation he said that he had never heard of the place, neither did he particularly want to know where it was. The men's delegates were duly shocked at the noble lord's ignorance.

The Agreement gave the docker his highest pay ever, two shillings an hour, with a guaranteed four hours' work and with two calls each day. The working week was limited to forty-four hours. Overtime payments fell into line. From then on 'work or maintenance' became the goal of the Federation. Lord Shaw had shied away from pronouncing on the practicability of the principle. He had been content to include the 'maintenance [of workers] during unemployment or under-employment' in the schedule of matters left over for further discussion. The principle did, at least, find honourable mention in this, the first of an almost unending record of enquiries into conditions of labour in the docks. A definite step forward was the appointment in each port of a Local Joint Committee, which tackled problems that had resisted solution within the dock walls. In London problems pertaining to the employment of PLA dockworkers were dealt with by the PLA Group Joint Committee. Two other Group Committees met to consider Short Sea Traders and Ocean Shipowners labour, where conditions were peculiar to these industries.

In the years immediately before the Second War, I was the Secretary of the PLA Committee that met regularly under the chairmanship of Robert (afterwards Sir Robert) Letch. The Committee prided itself on never having failed to find a solution to problems referred to it. This happy state of affairs lasted until after the Second War.

Before leaving the Shaw Award, paragraph 21 has sufficient historic interest to be quoted : 'No stoppage of work or lock-out shall take place locally, sectionally or otherwise, pending any matter being referred to and adjusted by a Local Committee, and such adjustment shall be accepted by both parties as final.' This paragraph has never been repealed nor officially repudiated. *No agreement to which both sides have subscribed, in the full panoply of mutual trust, has been so honoured in the committee room and so ignored in the docks.* The scant importance attached by the rank and file to agreements made by their representatives had an unhappy precedent in the strike of 1911. It has been the most disquieting feature of the decades since 1945; few official enquiries held during that period have failed to draw attention to the one-sided observance of agreements made with the unions.

In July 1920 Lord Devonport was successful in forming the National Association of Port Employers. From this time onwards the Association can be referred to as the 'Employers'. Likewise, Bevin was intent on straightening out the affairs of the Federation, of which the dockers had shared with lightermen, carmen and coal porters the services of the union officials. From his efforts emerged the Transport and General Workers Union; Bevin was now the rising star of the transport workers' world. He failed, however, to bring in the stevedores, whose Amalgamated Stevedors Protective League was the oldest organisation of labour in the port of London, dating from the 1840s. As the Amalgamated and United Societies of Stevedores it threw its weight in the 1889 struggle on the side of the dockers. After the General Strike of 1926 it opened its ranks to a number of dockers who felt that their interests had not been properly looked after by the massive T & GWU and it took the more comprehensive title of the National Amalgamated Stevedores and Dockers. This was a blow to the prestige of Bevin, and no further efforts on his part ever succeeded in bringing the members of the Stevedores Union into the T & GWU fold. Basically there was no answer to the superior status that one of the oldest customs of the port claimed for the shipworker. The enmity between the two unions, feebly masked by the fraternal modes of greeting laid down as being proper between organised workers, has been a main cause of labour stoppages from which the employers, largely helpless, have been the sufferers. Dictated by the cost of living which fell steeply as trade became depressed following the short-lived post-war boom, wages were reduced to 14s. a day in July 1921 and again, to 12s. in March 1922, dipping later to an all-time low of 11s. After a short but bitter strike in 1924 it reverted to 12s. In 1931 during the trough of the Depression it fell to 11s. 2d. a day from which it climbed gradually to 19s. in 1947.

Right The late Alfred C. White, with a background of African Mahogany logs. *Below* A valuable stock of Greenheart Logs from Central America—East Wood Wharf 1925.

Tea clippers in East India Docks, London, about 1890.

9

My return to the PLA in April 1919 had been helped by an unorthodox move I had employed while still working as a soldier clerk in the Shipping Department of the War Office. I had been sent there on leaving hospital, in 1917, as an alternative to being discharged as unfit for further service. Soon after the Armistice on being told that I should be needed in my present job for another twelve months, I thought that the PLA might have something to say. The Director of Movements, on my suggestion, wrote to Lord Devonport. It was the first time in the short history of the Authority that the attention of the Chairman had been drawn by name to the existence of so lowly a being as a Fourth Class Clerk. It made considerable impression on the Staff Department of the Head Office and for some time I was known as the 'young man the Chairman had a letter about', and this proved a great help.

Within a few weeks I was promoted to the Special Classification, a significant step out of the rut of General Classification, and for which competition was keen. On presenting myself for the interview, following a very simple written examination, I was impressed, as it was intended I should be, by the Board Room atmosphere that was part of the process of selection. At intervals along an oak table in the committee room into which the aspirants had been herded were large brass ashtrays for the use of Board Members. One of the sweating candidates lit a cigarette to steady his nerves. 'No smoking!' roared the Janitor, a Man Messenger imbued completely with the Head Office servility.

'What are the ashtrays for if we can't smoke?'

'Not for the likes of you,' came the crushing reply from the liveried sycophant. The incident was typical of the age and traditions of the dock company in whose service he had been bred. Appointed a Fourth Class Clerk, Special Classification, I was sent to the Commercial Department of the Head Office in Leadenhall Street. I took no part in the commerce of London. A cul-de-sac in the department dealt with Dues on Ships and Charges on Goods. I do not remember any of the responsible clerks attempting to teach me about matters with which the department dealt. Rates for racking wine, garbling nutmegs, whether Passing over Quay charge should be applied and where the London Clause began and ended, meant less to me than the Jabberwock. Now twenty-five years old I esimated my knowledge of practical dock work at about one per cent.

For two years I was in charge of the Department Register; my job was to number the new files and try hard not to lose the old ones. I learnt how impossible it is to index a subject so that it can be instantly located by someone else years later. No two people receive in their minds the same impact from an incident, nor are their impressions identical.

About that time a cigarette-end thrown by a careless clerk from the open window of a room on an upper floor of the Head Office landed in the rim of the bowler hat worn by an ex-commander of the Royal Navy. Incensed both at the damage to his hat and his dignity, he demanded, and received, from the General Manager the price of a new bowler hat. The file containing a report of the incident, and the correspondence, was duly put away and forgotten.

Incredible as it may seem, some years later another cigarette-end thrown from an upper window of the same building landed in the same way. The owner of the hat demanded, in person, compensation from the General Manager. Having an excellent memory and wishing to be guided by precedent, the file dealing with the earlier case was immediately called for. The register clerk was at lunch. To the growing irritation of a number of officials who were drawn into the search the papers could not be found. The owner of the hat had to be satisfied that he would be recompensed as soon as the previous papers could be located.

Hardly had the returning register clerk put his head inside the door than he was besieged by his colleagues. 'Those papers about the commander whose hat was damaged by a cigarette-end—

what are they filed under? We've looked under "C" for cigarette, "B" for bowler hat and "H" for hat. You're for the high jump if you haven't found them by the time the old man comes back from lunch.'

Imperturbably the register clerk referred to his ledger and from the appropriate cabinet extracted the file. His amazed fellow clerks clustered round, demanding to know the secret. 'What on earth letter is it filed under?'

' "I", of course. Irate old man's hat damaged by cigarette-end.'

As I listened to the hum of the department I saw that here again, was a parade being made of doing nothing when there was nothing doing, but, naturally, on a much higher scale than the docks could put on. It was inspired by the head of the department himself. At intervals the door of his private office flew open—it had no handle to give preliminary warning. Before it had time to shut, the draught of his passing swept the papers off my desk. A door in the distant corridor twanged in violent protest against his jet-propelled passage. His example was catching. I watched the Senior Canvasser, as staff of the Commercial Department were called, rush into the office, throw his hat and coat on to a chair, seize the telephone and demand that the operator cut off the unfortunate caller with whom a certain Dock Superintendent was at the time speaking. Open-mouthed I waited for an order, probably to empty the water out of the dock or shut down the dock itself, that would justify this panache. To my disappointment it was to enquire why there had been delay in despatching some grain sweepings for the Head's chickens and why had the work been allowed to interfere with this?

As the path of the junior clerk at the dock was blocked until he passed his swimming test, so the junior clerk at the Head Office had to satisfy the Authority, within six months of his appointment that he could take dictation at one hundred words a minute and, what was more important, transcribe his Pitman's shorthand correctly. The standard was high. Many returned warriors made half-hearted attempts at a subject where only complete concentration could ensure success. To pass a test at one hundred words a minute it was necessary to write fluently one hundred and fifty. The point the ex-soldiers made, quite wrongly, as they found on

71

being returned to the dock staff, was: 'They can't do that sort of thing to us.' They could and they did.

It did not take long to learn that all the sound and fury of the Commercial Department added up to very little. Even then I had a glimpse that the way the work was done by the dock officers must count for more with shipowners and traders than the smooth words of my well-dressed colleagues. Years later the then General Manager confirmed this. 'It's not your blue eyes will get the work, my boy—it's because the docks do it better than the wharves.' However, in suspecting this I was in a minority of one, and I looked round for a way out. It was now too late for the Civil Service and the first of the post-war depressions was causing many restless ex-soldiers to think again. My father had once told me that a man tends to become that which he thinks he is and I had no wish to drift into becoming a City gent. I had an obsession to know how the work in the docks was done; I listened with awe to the very occasional dock officer who visited the department. With the confidence born of youth and complete ignorance of the task I was setting myself, I decided that I would learn all that there was to be known about dock operating and that I would become a Dock Superintendent. Among the many thousands of staff there were only five of these and they formed the narrow apex of the broadly based staff pyramid; they were the friends and confidants of the management. It took exactly thirty years to achieve my ambition. Nearly fifty years after I am still learning about port operating with little chance of knowing all that there is to be known. In time I saw that the more knowledge one acquires of dock work the more hesitant one becomes to claim infallibility. Practices vary with ports, progress is continuous, even dock terms have different meanings, and the outlook on ship turnround is quite different in many ports abroad. During the Second War a subaltern who confounded all my theories was sent to me in Italy. Noticing from his papers that he had been a hairdresser and wondering how, even in wartime, the War Office had regarded this knowledge as likely to be an asset to a Port Operating Group, I asked him what he knew about dock work. Without a qualm, he said: 'Oh, I know all about docks and ports, sir. I had a fortnight's training at Longmoor.' This was the centre of the Royal Engineers, Transportation. Over the main entrance was inscribed, so it was said, 'Those who know do, those who don't know, teach.' After a time he became a useful officer.

In 1921 I threw away all the gentlemanly amenities of the Head Office and secured promotion to the rank of 'Second Class Assistant Warehousekeeper', the lowest form of life in the traffic and operating grade and equivalent to the army rank of subaltern. The Selection Committee took under one minute to point out that I knew nothing about the work of the docks and yet I was offering myself as one seeking authority there. To this I had nothing to say. Fortunately for me the Chairman remarked : 'My boy, you know nothing of dock work—never mind, you'll learn. I like your chin.'

I have always thought of this as an early and instinctively sound method of personnel selection. Once more a simple job done in a simple way.

My last recollection of Leadenhall Street was the opening by King George V of the dock to which he gave his name. It was a lovely summer day and the ceremony will be long remembered. Never again will so many top hats be seen in and around the shipping centre of the City.

In Field Service Regulations the young Army officer is advised that 'time spent on reconnaissance is seldom wasted'. What I saw of the Wood Wharves, my new department, on a preliminary visit made me regret the cosy atmosphere of the City office. As far as the eye could see there were stacks of logs—huge mahogany logs, some weighing as much as ten tons. Steam cranes belching out smoke and steam trundled along railway lines, a log swaying from each jib. It looked to me to be a very dangerous place. Men were shooting cumbersome trucks, loaded high with logs, up the shed alleyways, by ropes worked from the many capstans on the quay. Turntables at the entrance to each shed were grinding round with their loaded trucks by the same skilled manipulation of rope and capstan. In the background were barges filled with more logs and many with cut timber—lumber as I afterwards learnt that it was called. The department consisted of several sets of sheds, the water spaces being connected with bridges. As I watched, two men inserted a long iron handle amidships and a bridge began clumsily to move to allow a loaded barge to pass through the cutting. The all-round picture seemed rather primitive but with a great deal of latent power. Actually I was watching the most highly mechanised department at that time in the port, with its high capital investment which included overhead gantry cranes in the twenty-eight log sheds. I could not fail to notice in all this activity an absence of noise and confusion. Every man appeared to know his job and to be doing it quietly and efficiently. As I got to know more about the work of a port I was to learn that the more noise the less efficiency. When I reported to the Dock Superintendent his only advice to me was: 'You please Mr White [the head of the department] and you'll please me.'

My immediate job was not, however, at the huge Meccano set of the East Wood Wharf that I had watched the previous day, but at the West Wood Wharf, half a mile away and separated by the Rum Quay, an ancient part of the dock which I was to know intimately at a later stage. My charge had then quite a large area at the Limehouse end of the West India Dock. Abutting on the Rum Quay were three heavily built sheds equipped with hand-operated overhead gantries for piling smaller types of logs than the East Wood Wharf handled. The gantries ran parallel across the shed; each month they were serviced by an ex-sailor, Davy Wood, who although a heavily built man of over sixty, leapt nimbly across the five-feet space that separated the heavy cross beams rather than climb down the ladder and up the adjacent one. A feature of 'upstairs' were the chalk records that had lasted for so many years. They recorded the minor happenings of what was normally a quiet and not very active dock department. 'Mike Leary and Sam Evans walked across the dock on the ice, February 1895', 'Dave Regan picked up a rosewood log weighing four hundredweight', 'Joe Spencer went into the dock after a carman, October 1900'.

Two of the more modern sheds overlooked the main road and gave on to the Lower Pool. Late on a Saturday afternoon in 1921 I saw Shackleton's *Discovery* leaving the Thames for her Antarctic voyage. There was always something to watch on the West Ferry Road; traffic was still mainly horse drawn. One afternoon, hearing shouts and cries that were certainly not caused by an English crowd, I discovered, coming round the bend in the road, what looked like an outsized and tinselly wedding cake, carried on poles, by four Indian seamen. Some hundreds more seamen, many carrying replicas of the wedding cake, were dancing and running in and out. Crude musical instruments gave a background to the

74

general cacophony. What was the idea of this colourful procession in this drab part of London?

'That's Hobson-Jobson, that is—every year about this time, they go barmy over it. Mind you, they don't do no harm. When there's been a lot of ships in with native crews, I've seen hundreds taking part.' This was from my foreman, a man with a lifetime at the West India Docks; he thought it might be a celebration of the Mohammedan Festival of Mohurram. He was quite right. As late as 1968, 'Hobson-Jobson, a Glossary of Anglo-Indian words and phrases' by Henry Yale and A. C. Burnell was published. This gives Hobson-Jobson as the British soldier's idea of Mohammedan cries of 'Ya Hasan-Ya Hosain' at the festival of Mohurram. Ex-soldiers from the Indian Army, turned dockers, must have recognised it.

Like many another trade, 'dye and fancy woods' has been almost demolished both by fashions in furniture and by synthetic dyes and plastics. Part of my territory was taken up by logwood from the Spanish Isthmus; for three hundred years this had been the main source of purple and black dyes. The sober tastes of the Puritans had given it an enhanced value. Growing on the slopes of the Spanish Main, it was cut, barked and loaded on to mule trains for shipment to Spain. Two generations earlier the gold and silver trains had attracted Drake in these waters. The buccaneers of the seventeenth century are not so well known and logwood has not the allure of gold and silver. Precious it was, however, and many lives were lost before the Spaniards allowed foreigners a share in this lucrative trade.

Another wood imported, for insecticides, was quassia. This came in logs of fairly soft wood and they were ground into chips, which, with water added, gave off a sharp and acrid smell. Plastics have now largely replaced the beautiful woods imported in the 1920s, such as tulip, kingwood, lignum vitae, Macassar ebony, East Indian rosewood, snakewood and Amboyna burrs—these have disappeared altogether from modern furniture design. The rosewood piano, the tulip wood vase that made an elegant match for the Cuban mahogany wardrobe, are relics of a gracious life that was lived half a century ago. How long is it since a snakewood walking stick has been seen on a fine morning in Pall Mall?

Much of the work at the West Wood Wharf consisted of landing, measuring and piling many thousand pieces of cut oak and mahogany. This was, perhaps, the most detailed and deliberate process to which any important commodity was subjected. Timber measurers, a relic of the old dock company's staff, conducted these operations in an impeccable manner. Over the years the complete impartiality of the dock measurers had been established. Added to this was their incorruptibility, a valuable asset in a trade with many soiled tassels on its fringe. The measurement accounts issued by the PLA had come to have the value of documents of title. I discovered this when the total cubic feet of a parcel of oak was swollen by the measurer inadvertently adding the date. The importer represented that he had paid the shipper on our figures which he had come to regard as being above suspicion. Rather than quibble over the discrepancy the Authority paid up and preserved the inviolability of their accounts.

The West Wood Wharf was an ideal place for a young officer to learn his trade. With a staff of about a dozen experts and labourers that rarely rose above the fifty mark during busy times, the work, although complicated, seldom became as hectic as was common at the nearby ship discharging departments. Prior to my arrival an entirely new set of piecework rates had been agreed. This was part of a general revision of piecework rates made by the PLA so as to bring them into line with the recent Shaw Award. Unfortunately, the schedule agreed for the Wood Wharves was basically unsound. It provided for a weekly piecework bill for all the various gangs working on the department and it ran into many hundred hours. It would have been unsound at any department at which it had been applied. Piecework implies that each man engaged works to the utmost of his ability. This he will do for as long as he is convinced that the other men on the piecework bill are working equally hard. The bill must cover the work of a gang that will allow of this; eleven men working as a ship discharging gang will satisfy these conditions. To encourage output, the time covered by the bill must be limited. If a gang meets with adverse conditions during the first few hours of their bill, such as bad weather or mechanical breakdowns, an appropriate allowance can be made and the bill, which is for eight hours only, can be made to pay. If, however, the bill covers a week's work, it may be dragged down (and the fact is known by all the men it covers) by bad conditions during the first day or two. Thus there are two requisites without which piecework will prove a failure : a gang where each man can keep his eye on his fellow workers, and a bill that is sufficiently short to be written off when conditions are unfavourable. The week's bill for the rambling area known as the West Wood Wharf fell down badly on both these counts. After a year of 'fiddling' with the weekly bill in an attempt to provide a reasonable surplus, the system was scrapped in favour of daily gang bills. I remember, to take one instance, that a gang measuring mahogany boards at the very poor rate of four loads a day, suddenly jumped to thirteen loads on finding that its earnings were in its own hands. If the best employer is, as Henry Ford remarked, the one that can *contrive* to pay the highest wages, then it was a good day's work for the Authority when the cumbersome system of weekly bills was scrapped.

The ethics of piecework were not the only ones to which I was introduced at the West Wood Wharf. Certain timber merchants imported large quantities of cut timber which they sold on, or before, landing and which was delivered from the quay at reduced handling charges. One such merchant who was having difficulty in disposing of his cargo and could see a sizeable balance lapsing on to full charges, asked me to go with him from my office to the place where his timber was still being landed. After deploring his bad fortune and the injustice of the Authority's charges he pulled out a gold cigarette-case; turning his back on me he offered me a cigarette. On one side of the case, among four cigarettes lay a neatly rolled £5 note, a week's money in 1922. On my remarking that I did not smoke he reluctantly returned the case to his pocket.

I O

After a two years' apprenticeship at the West Wood Wharf I graduated to the business end of the department, the East Wood Wharf. Here I had the good fortune to work directly with the warehousekeeper, Mr A. White. An officer from the Surrey Commercial Docks Company, his outlook and training had been totally different from those of his present colleagues from the London and India Docks Company. For some years prior to his transfer to the West India Dock he had been in charge of the floated timber department where he had had as independent a command as any dock could provide. As a result he had developed a 'fine disregard for the rules of the game'. Unlike most dock officers he welcomed responsibility, never hesitated to give a decision and thereafter stuck to it. He rarely sought higher authority for his actions. As these were based on long experience of timber handling and knowledge of human nature, they invariably turned out successfully. Just before my arrival he had thrown the dock management into confusion by deciding to put a complete cargo of mahogany logs into the dock water, there to be rafted by men he had brought from his old department. At the time there was neither room on the quays to land this cargo nor craft into which it could be put. To pond it was a sensible solution, and the qualms of the Dock Superintendent at seeing a job of this magnitude done in a way outside his experience and the fears of the Dockmaster who foresaw queues of ships with propellers broken on logs that had come adrift from the rafts, proved groundless. Sensing that it was going to be a success, the management, on being appealed to, said simply: 'Leave White alone, he knows what he is doing.' These few words epitomised his handling of his department and in fact, in the unforgiving and intensely practical world of the docks no higher praise could ever be given, or sought, than 'he knows what he is doing'. Bred in the traditions of the Surrey Docks he spoke his mind and was incapable of a shady action either to his staff or to the men in his charge. The sound pieces of advice he gave me were to stand me in good stead. In an argument with a shipping company over a shortage of timber, I had drafted a letter for his signature. After careful study of the problem I had got them well and truly sewn up and without a leg to stand on. Tossing the letter back to me unsigned, he said : 'I shouldn't send that if I were you. All you say is one hundred per cent true but it will leave a stink behind you. Maybe one of the staff will let *you* down before long and then you'll have to go and ask a favour from them. How will you feel then?' After a few words on the telephone the matter was settled to the satisfaction of both parties and with goodwill unimpaired. I thought of this action of his many years later when I read what Lord Beaverbrook said : 'If you have all the cards in your hands, remember that the other man has to go back to his boss. Don't strip him naked as no doubt you could do. Leave him with a few shreds of clothing.'

In those days admitting an error was thought, and with some reason, to condemn the member of the staff concerned. After White had spent some time in proving that one of our staff was at fault, he turned to me and said : 'Why don't these fellows have the common sense to realise that when you have made a mistake your best defence is to admit it honestly? Nobody can kick a man who admits he's wrong. If you're a twister and give the boss the trouble of proving you're not only a fool to make the mistake but a liar in not admitting it, you'll deserve all you get.'

I did not have long to wait to prove how valuable this advice could be. During my Principal's absence on leave a partner in a timber firm of repute whose headquarters were in Liverpool came to London to mark three logs that were to be cross cut immediately for shipment to Spain. Together we looked at the logs which he identified by marking them with chalk; he asked that we would start the cross cutting at 8 a.m. the following morning. The order for the work would reach the department by the first post. This it did and revealed to my consternation that the first of the three logs which we had just finished cutting in half did not belong to the

Liverpool merchant. In his haste he had not properly identified it the previous afternoon; on the department we did not know, unless the ledgers told us, to whom logs belonged. We were at fault in commencing the job, the most irrevocable of any on a log department, before we had written confirmation. The only way out was to ask the merchant to buy the log from its owner before the latter discovered that his log had, without his knowledge, been cut in half. Had the bush telegraph worked, and the Wood Wharves were alive with timber merchants, many of whom had offices in the departmental block, the value would have rocketed. Fortunately the owner was deservedly the most unpopular man in the trade and no one passed the word to him. Later that day I met the merchant who had hurried down from Liverpool. I put all my cards on the table and accepted responsibility for the expense to which he had been put. He immediately absolved the department of all blame and together we had a look at the 'wrong' log. Not even the most experienced timber merchant can see inside a log. How a log will open up remains unpredictable. This proved to be an excellent log in every way. When we put the saw across the log we *should* have cut I noticed a look of concern on the faces of the two men operating the crosscut saw. One of them picked up a handful of the sawdust and offered it to the merchant. It was pap and denoted something very wrong with the texture of the log. Later in the cutting the saw bit once more. The cross section revealed a two-inch belt of pap wood, caused by a dying down of the tree for several years, followed by a coming to life again and a resumption of normal growth. A most unusual phenomenon that would, had the log been shipped to the customer, have been a bad let-down all round.

Logs are temperamental cargo. The dock practice is to weigh each log separately, charges being assessed on gross weight. The importer employs a rough check on the dock weights, by converting from his known measurement. Some of the larger African mahogany trees will produce five or six logs, each of seven to ten tons in weight and each scribed with the tree number followed by the log or cut number. On my desk one morning was a letter from a log importer pointing out that we had returned the weights of two logs that were consecutive cuts from the same tree and both within a few cubic feet in their contents, but with more than a ton difference in their weights. As these would be known in the trade as 'sister' logs the discrepancy was certainly due to bad weighing; they would expect a refund of the charges that had been incorrectly made. 'What do we do now?' I asked my chief who had had a long experience of being let down by weighing and tally clerks. 'We could try writing to Liverpool and asking the receiver there if he would be kind enough to have them put over the weighbridge when they arrive—it's just a chance.' A week later we had a reply enclosing the certified weight slips that confirmed our weighings. What incident in the life of a giant tree in a faraway African forest had caused so grave a discrepancy between two adjacent parts, we shall never know.

The incident taught me not to give up too soon. Many years later, by refusing to accept the evidence of a complete range of marks and numbers, I was able to prove that cases that had been shipped with duplicate marks and numbers had been stolen from the dock, whilst apparently leaving the parcel intact.

A junior officer with his mind fixed on promotion did not consider himself to be educated until he had learned to bear up under misfortunes that, in the course of business, occasionally brought about the downfall of a senior officer. In the very early days of his career each officer provided himself with an up-to-date list of officers, on each of the grades superior to his own. Some were known to have a companion list showing the year and the month when each of these was due to retire. To brush away a tear with one hand whilst with the other reaching for the promotion list was the normal reaction from a healthy young officer. Lowliness was still young ambition's ladder; while there's death there's hope was a comforting philosophy.

In 1924 came an early attempt to mechanise the handling of logs at the Wood Wharves. No one who watched the failure of this crude experiment saw anything of the potent force that two decades and another major war away would produce a silent revolution in cargo handling. All the logs at the East Wood Wharf were transported on heavy rail flats. To turn these into the shed gangways, whence each log could be picked up by an overhead gantry, the wagon was 'turned' on a wooden turntable, worked by capstans and ropes. There were more than fifty of these turntables on the department and many were in need of replacement. In an effort to avoid the heavy expense a suggestion came from the Head Office (rumour had it that it was directly from the General Manager) that logs could be dragged individually by a tractor, thus gradually allowing the expensive turntables to go out of use. The suggestion was damned, firstly because it came from the Head Office and secondly, because no timber merchant would allow any of his logs to be dragged over the rough surface of the unpaved shed, where it would have collected loose stones and grit, a real menace to the sawmill; this was an understandable and reasonable objection. However, as the General Manager proposed to witness the experiment, we 'found' a log whose ownership had always been a departmental mystery, and all was ready for the day. Watched by the party of Head Office 'experts' and also several pessimistic merchants, the log was dogged on to the towing bar of the tractor, the driver of which hauled it obediently down the length of a typical shed gangway. Ordered to bring it back again the driver sat there looking puzzled. The majority of the log sheds were cul-de-sacs and the driver had jammed himself, his tractor and the pendant log in an end position from which he could be extricated only by the overhead traveller. Disgustedly the General Manager called off the experiment, discouraged by the lack of enthusiasm shown by the timber trade, as well as by the practical difficulties, of which he had not the grace to admit that he had had prior warning. That was the end of mechanisation at the Wood Wharves.

A last recollection of the department was the opportunity to discharge a sailing ship that had arrived with a cargo of Cuban mahogany logs, after a voyage lasting forty-eight days. She was the last sailing vessel, apart from the occasional firewood ship from Scandinavia, to be discharged in the West India Docks. I think she must have been the last vessel to make use of the 'lay days'. This was a period free of dues, granted to sailing ships by the PLA. It was also the last relic of the conditions before the bustle that steam brought into the docks. On going on board and telling the Master that I would start the discharge at 1 p.m. he immediately claimed his lay day. Work on the cargo had to be postponed while he made a leisurely report to his owners in the City. The direct connection that existed between the ship and her cargo and the Captain was another casualty that steam brought. The modern ship is increasingly becoming a mere steel box that can be propelled from A to B with a regularity that makes possible sailing schedules for months ahead. Gone now is the sense of achievement that was felt when the perils of nature, plus the King's Enemies, had been safely surmounted. A Bill of Lading that passed through my hands in 1912 at the London Docks—it had been issued for a parcel of spices, carried by a sailing ship and was couched in the language of Elizabeth I—concluded with the prayer : 'And now may God bring the good ship in safety to her Haven, Amen.' Those days, less than sixty years ago, were nearer to the coracle age than to the container stage of today.

I I

During the four years I spent at the Wood Wharves I had pieced together some of the history of dock labour. Knowledgeable members of the staff had outlined for me the brief history that had led to the formation of the PLA in 1909. I was surrounded also by busy general cargo departments where I took a vicarious interest in the complex work of discharging and loading ships. I was particularly absorbed by the difficult task that my colleagues faced daily in penetrating the jungle of dock labour.

In 1802 the West India Dock, the first of the enclosed system of docks that make up the port of London, was opened for ships. A labour force of 200 permanent men was appointed by the Directors. These were recruited from the 'Mudlarks' who discharged cargo ships berthed at the buoys in the River Thames. For practical reasons which will be gone into later, this number was soon reduced; reliance was, thereafter, placed on casual labour. The nucleus of permanent men probably stood at about ten per cent of the fluctuating daily labour force. The unfortunate pattern that economic necessity imposed on this, the earliest of the many dock companies, continued until it became substantially part of the latest major London port construction, the King George V Dock, opened in 1921.

During a period of 160 years, from the time when the varied work of the docker was first recognised as an industry, the seeds of its own tragedy have been present. Scarcity of labour during the Napoleonic wars produced an hourly rate of $5\frac{1}{2}d$. After Waterloo this fell to $4\frac{1}{2}d$.; by 1828, when the St Katharine Docks were opened, men were paid $4d$. It remained at this low figure until 1872; a few years of trade prosperity, coinciding with the birth of

Above   Frozen-out dock labourers at London Docks, 1855.
Below   Dockers at Royal Docks awaiting 'call on', 1962.

Forklift truck picking up a cased motor car.

the first dockers' unions, pushed it up to 5d. Not until the notorious stoppage of 1889—a struggle led by John Burns for the Dockers' Tanner—were the employers forced to concede one halfpenny an hour more than had been paid in 1802. The first struggle in 1911 between labour and the new Port of London Authority set a wage of 7d.

It took the First War to bring rewards for labour to a figure comparable with other major industries and in 1920 the docker enjoyed what to him appeared to be the fabulous sum of 2s. per hour. Needless to say this largesse failed to outlast the boom of the next few years and a series of reductions followed. The Depression of 1931 reduced the rate to 1s. 4½d. As the rearmament boom set the pattern of international trade, the dockers' wage rose to 1s. 7½d. As a concession to the rising cost of living increases, it was fixed at 2s. 4½d. Since then it has been increased continually until it stands (1968) at 6s. 6½d.[1] The figures quoted are for the nationally agreed basic hourly rate. *They take no account of piece-work or overtime earning.*

Dock work has always consisted of alternate slumps and booms. As the days of the week go by there is never the same demand for portworkers; in the port of Liverpool, recently, there were 9,000 fewer dockers required on two successive days. Faced with these conditions, which were the norm for all major ports, how could realistic employers, with shareholders to satisfy, apply utterly un-realistic schemes of decasualisation? It was not until 1940, under pressure of the Second War, that the industry accepted a measure of responsibility for the well-being of its workers during periods of enforced unemployment. Although this move salved the national conscience, it did not tackle the deep-seated problem of casual labour.

Not until 1967 was this Utopia, for which thousands had fought for six generations of workers, achieved. The joy with which the Press and the Unions hailed the government-assisted revolution was soon turned to exasperation by an unofficial stoppage of work that spread to most of the U.K. ports, paralysed vital export work-ing for six weeks and precipitated the devaluation of sterling. The

[1] See Appendix A for a detailed picture of the depressed labour payments during the nineteenth century.

Unions played an ineffective part; no one expected more from them.

The two post-war decades had seen a dreary record of broken agreements, stoppages, go-slows, refusals of overtime working and major strikes. These put the dockers well to the top of the industrial disputes league and brought into prominence many of the minor ports.[1] A silent revolution in cargo handling methods had, over the same period, been taking place. Out of the Second War came the mechanical appliances that the U.S. Forces took with them to the various theatres of war and which they generously shared with their Allies. The forklift truck, the pallet and the mobile crane formed a combination of cargo handling appliances having a future limited only by the ingenuity of the port operator.

Gone for ever was the custom dating before the time of Henry II, when wool was shipped from South Coast ports in exchange for the wine of Bordeaux and the brandy of Charente. Never again would every unit of cargo be prepared so that it could be manhandled. The reason was that only at one stage in the process of landing cargo from, or loading cargo into, a ship was it likely that a crane, or the ships' gear, would be available. For the remaining stages as between the plantation, or the manufacturers' premises, and those of the receiver, the goods were lifted, rolled or pitched, often by porters working under most primitive conditions. Cargo that could not be treated in such a way was an expensive exception that delayed normal ship work and was, where possible, avoided.

Now that the port operator could mechanically handle cargo there was an international movement towards increasing the size and the weight of the cargo unit, until the container (weighing up to 30 tons) became the normal unit on certain trade routes. The complex agreements between port users by which this desirable end was achieved will be dealt with later. A recent economic survey[2] has estimated that *ninety per cent of the present strength of dockworkers will not be required within the next decade* to

[1] Harwich, Felixstowe, Shoreham and Margate have all taken traffic from the major ports.
[2] The McKinsey Report of 1967, prepared for British Rail Docks Division.

handle the present (or an increased) tonnage, when it is shipped in containers or in bulk form.

However much this prediction was played down at the time it will remain substantially true. Within a year of the publication of the McKinsey Report inducements are being held out to dockworkers, many of whom so recently gained a permanent position after years of casual work, to seek alternative employment. On Friday, August 30th, 1968 the first batch of men under 65 received sums of up to £2,000 each for leaving the service of the PLA.[1] The building and operation of special berths at Tilbury Docks for container ships has led the PLA in 1968 reluctantly to close the London and St Katharine Docks, twenty-six miles away. The nearby Regent's Canal Dock will go shortly. As part of the general pattern, because container traffic must be international to survive, every maritime country is now agitating to replace the general cargo package with the largest practical cargo unit. The shipping industry has seen more changes in two decades than in the previous thirty centuries. These changes are by no means yet completed; it is certain that the dockers will be the major casualty.

Had decasualisation been imposed on the industry twenty years ago it would have benefited the very large number of workers required to handle through the war-battered ports the unprecedented demand for consumer goods. Mechanisation was then in its empiric infancy; too soon to talk about the savings in labour that this would herald.

Had decasualisation been postponed for another ten years it would have been meaningless. By then the small number of dockers still required to work the remaining general cargo that had defied unit handling could easily have been found from the nucleus of permanent men from a staff already eroded by redundancies and pensioning.

---

[1] The London Docks Modernisation Committee announced (April 1968) that there were at least 2,750 men more than were needed in the port.

I 2

I have, so far, set out in its stark essentials the tragedy that is being enacted in the ports of this country. It is general to all the major world ports; the more advanced they are in their working methods the more quickly will disaster come. The conditions in which the docker has always worked need to be appreciated because they are without parallel in industry or in agriculture. I shall first describe how the major dock systems in the port of London came to be built and how their struggles to survive left the employers with no alternative to the brutal conditions of casual labour. The Great Strike of 1889 produced the hitherto unknown advantages of group organisation and first glimpsed the immense power of union loyalty, which eighty years later, gave the grandsons of the strikers their permanent jobs. It will be necessary also to describe the typical daily working conditions applicable to the more than one hundred vessels that the PLA accommodate in their five dock systems. The work on the ships in each of these is dominated by the twice-daily tides, a further variant from the assembly line of the factory. To simplify the story I shall confine the account of labour developments to dockers employed within the docks of the PLA. This will exclude workers in other ports and also those that work at the wharves and riverside premises in the port of London.

As international trade increased towards the end of the eighteenth century pressure on the facilities of London as a port produced conditions little short of scandalous. Sailing ships by the hundred, laden with sugar, timber, tea and other valuable commodities, were moored in tiers in the open river below London Bridge. Apart from the damage caused by storms and floating ice, pilferage by shipworkers and others is reputed to have removed as much as thirty per cent of the cargoes. Neither the importers nor the government could stand this. The removal from the river moorings in 1802 of all ships carrying sugar (in hogsheads) from the West Indies to the West India Docks gave protection to the ships, a constant water level and secure conditions where the Revenue could collect the ever-increasing duties by which Pitt paid for the Napoleonic wars. The proprietors of this dock built huge warehouses for sugar and accommodation for the long-term storage of rum and timber, all making necessary the employment of a large body of workers. This was the pattern followed at the London Docks (opened 1805) and repeated at the St Katharine Docks opened in 1828. Both of these docks,[1] within a mile of London Bridge, did not cater for more than the small ships of the period and were consequently at a disadvantage after the 1850s, when the necessity to carry many tons of coal caused the early steamships to leap ahead, both in length and draught. In 1855 the Victoria Dock set the pattern for dock systems, which from their distance from the City of London became known as the 'lower docks'. They were essentially transit docks. This meant that the ever-increasing cargoes of valuable merchandise from the Far East, Africa and America had to be sent by barge or rail to the 'upper docks' where there were warehouses with conditions acceptable to the Crown. In 1864 the London, St Katharine and the Victoria Docks Companies amalgamated to form the London and St Katharine Docks Company; the proprietors, in 1880, built the Albert Dock as an extension seawards of the Victoria Dock, which gave an outlet to the Thames at Woolwich. The London Company now had two major down-stream docks on whose cargoes they could draw to keep their warehouses full and an ever-increasing number of dockers employed.

To serve the ships of the Honourable East India Company complete with adequate warehouses, in 1806 the smaller East India Dock had been built. In 1838 it merged with the neighbouring West India Docks to form the East and West India Docks Company. With the praiseworthy intention of providing cargo to keep its warehouses filled, the company bought land for more docks at Tilbury, twenty-six miles below London Bridge. The failure of this

[1] In 1884 the average size of vessels entering what is now the Surrey Commercial Docks was not more than 344 tons deadweight.

new giant in construction, recognition of whose value under the conditions of the container age has had to wait for eighty years, caused, in 1889 a joining up of the two companies, who had for decades been rivals for the trade coming to London. The result of this unfortunate marriage of convenience, the London and India Docks Joint Committee, lasted for twelve years, the most sterile period in the history of London's port. Following the Great Strike of the same year the volume of trade fell into a static period; no part of the organisation suffered more than the workers in the port. The Joint Committee came to an unlamented end on January 1st, 1901, being replaced by the London and India Docks Company; their efforts to rationalise the employment of casual labour will be described later.

Meanwhile in 1868 the Millwall Docks had opened, mainly for European traffic. Cashing in on the importation of grain from the developing American and Canadian prairies, the dock attracted a new element in dock labour—the cornporters, more colloquially known as 'toe-rags', from their habit of binding their feet in sacking to protect them against the heated grain. Throughout the nineteenth century, on the south side of the Thames the Surrey Commercial Docks had been forming, through the amalgamation of various small dock and canal companies. Without an overall plan of any kind and restrained only by the curve of the River Thames, this dock of 365 acres grew into an 'irregular congerie of docks, cuttings and ponds'.[1] Nevertheless, it was the most prosperous of the Victorian docks, with an extensive business in European softwoods, grain and whaling. To handle the timber from an armada of small vessels that cleared from Baltic and Russian ports during the ice-free season, there had been formed a force of 'dealporters'. The conditions of their employment will be described later.

While dock companies had been striving with varying success to earn dividends for their shareholders, depressing labour and staff in the process, the state of the River Thames, the artery that guaranteed the flow of shipping to the five large controls and the hundreds of riverside wharves, had become badly clotted. The dredging and conservation programmes of the Thames Conservancy were hopelessly inadequate to cope with the ever-growing

[1] History of the Port of London—Sir Joseph Broodbank 1922.

size and draught of ships. In 1909 the Port of London Authority was formed; the undertakings of the Millwall and the Surrey Commercial Docks Companies, together with the London and India Docks Company, were absorbed into the framework of the new corporative authority. Certain duties were also taken over from the Thames Conservancy.

Major dock construction, leaving out the important developments taking place (1968) at Tilbury Docks for the container, packaged timber and bulk grain traffics, came to a halt in 1921 with the opening of the King George V Dock. This had been designed prior to the First War and was sited south of the Royal Albert Dock, making, with the Royal Victoria Dock, the largest enclosed dock area in the world. It soon became known as the 'Royal Group'.

This brief account of the century and a half's growth of the port of London will have shown how the unorganised mudlarks who worked ships during the French Revolution had grown through the many phases demanded by specialised commercial developments into the closed shop that port working became in 1941. As the advancing civilisation of the Victorian era entailed higher standards of living, imports grew in tonnage and variety. The volume of exports that helped to pay for them grew also. The dockworkers improved in their craft skills until they became expert in the processing of sugar, grain, dried fruits, tobacco, tea, wool, timber (both hardwood and softwood), wines and spirits and the more exotic items that figured in the rate books of the dock companies, such as ivory, spices, indigo and ostrich feathers. The growth of these specialist workers has often been a catalyst in the labour relations of the port.

The excellent intentions of the earlier dock companies to employ only permanent staff were defeated by the great handicap of the uncertain arrival of shipping. Sailing vessels were dependent on the prevailing winds. A period of contrary winds could keep a dock empty for weeks whilst an armada of vessels huddled together in the Downs waiting for the change of wind that would take them the few miles up the estuary and into the docks. In so far as steamships were independent of the wind there was some improvement but this was gradual and was not felt until the latter part of the century. Before a ship could keep her scheduled dates of arrival everything had to go right during a voyage that meant calling at many ports before London was reached. Storms and fogs were the main enemies as they still are. Political causes cannot be ignored either.[1]

The dock companies were, as men of business, keenly aware of the value of permanent labour. The vatting of rum and wines, the bulking of tea, the sorting and measurement of logs and lumber were typical of the jobs that they increasingly accepted as London developed into the world's largest commodity market. To cope with these and many similar tasks required an expert skill that was not to be found among the casually employed. The West India Docks Company started with 200, the London Docks Company with 100, increased in 1809 to 300, and the St Katharine Docks Company with 225 permanent men.[2] The first economies that were not long in coming took the form of a cut in permanent labour and a greater reliance on casual labour. The skills were there although exercised by casual men, recently downgraded from permanent status. In the 1870s, a prosperous time for the port, there is mention of 3,000 men being employed at London Docks; this fell to 500 when the dock was empty. These employees were permanent men and were engaged in warehousing and delivery work. Had there been a pool of labour or a workable plan between the various companies to transfer surplus labour against an unexpected demand from another dock, some of the suffering that was accepted as part of the dockers' way of life would have been avoided. As it was, every calling-on place was besieged, save in the occasional good times, by a crowd of applicants; every calling-on place had its margin of the disappointed. When trade increased exaggerated reports spread of work available at the docks. Unemployed agricultural workers, large numbers from Ireland, flooded into the East End of London where jobs could, it was reported, be had without credentials of any kind.

[1] The closure of the Suez Canal in 1956 and again in 1967, caused a delay of some weeks in the arrival of ships in London from the Far East and Australia.
[2] 'Honesty and sobriety are indispensable qualifications, the slightest deviation from them will be attended with immediate and irrevocable dismissal'—this was demanded by the St Katharine Docks Company in its initial recruitment of labour. For this they paid 4d. against the London Docks' 5½d. per hour.

'A hook' (to help in the handling of bales and cases), 'a bob' (for the taking-on foreman) 'and a four-letter name' (that the foreman could write in his book on a wet morning) were the essentials that the lucky ones were expected to produce. When Lloyd George's Insurance Act made necessary the carrying of individual named cards, the real names of dockworkers, often polysyllabic, were recorded for the first time.

Opinions naturally differ on work prospects during the first three-quarters of the nineteenth century. Sir Joseph Broodbank quotes an employer thus : 'The majority of dockers get as much work as they want and the most casual candidate has more work open to him than the hop picker, the herring curer or the number of seasonal trades centred in London.' He added : 'The men on the whole are a steady and honest class of worker, especially having regard to their opportunities for pilfering both food and drink.'

It is doubtful if the author of this rather complacent statement ever saw the daily struggles for the few hours' work offered. Henry Mayhew, the investigator of social conditions in Victorian England, gives a different picture. He spent some time watching the twice-daily calls, although his investigations were not welcomed by the dock companies. He tells of a timber porter, a farmer's son from Dorset, who 'had 14s. a week sometimes; many's the week I've had three and more's the week I've had nothing at all. I've lived on penny loaves, one or two a day and when there was no work then I've begged.' In one week in 1861, 42 ships berthed in the London Docks, in the next 131, in the next 209 and in the next only 29. When the winds at last relented 'then there is family rejoicing and such a feast that the frying pan is in requisition'—a grim barometer indeed of the social outlook.

With these conditions, and they were by no means abnormal, how could the management plan an orderly sequence of work? How could the casual labourer 'save, or earn the indulgence of his landlord against the inevitable harassment of rent which cannot be paid'?

By 1860 a permanent man was earning 16s. 6d. a week; by 1889 this had advanced to 18s. From this sum it was expected that 'he should become a steady saver'.

Mayhew has left an imperishable picture of a call, typical of any that took place at the docks. Conditions as late as the 1930s had not, to my recollection, substantially altered. In the winter of 1934 I remember leaving the West India Docks, after working all night, at about 5.30 a.m. It was a cold and wet morning. By the main gate in a shelter which had only a roof, but with a latrine on which men balanced themselves on a pole, were some fifty men waiting patiently and with hardly a sound until the call, then some two hours distant. Uncertain of work they felt that by stealing a march on later arrivals, they might be the lucky ones to get a morning's employment. From the many that were called few indeed were chosen; it was a pathetic sight that I have never forgotten.

Mayhew mentions that from 6 a.m., winter and summer, masses of men congregated around the principal entrances to the docks: 'some in half-fashioned surtouts, burst at the elbow, with the dirty shirts showing through; others in greasy sporting jackets, with red pimpled faces, others in rags of gentility; some in rusty black, others with the knowing thieve's curl on each side of the jaunty cap; here and there a big whiskered Pole. As the foreman made his appearance began the scuffling and scrambling forth of many hands, high in the air. All were shouting, appealing, coaxing. The scene is one to sadden the most callous with thousands of men struggling for one day's hire, the struggle being fiercer from the knowledge that hundreds must be left to idle the day out in want.'

In spite of the steady rise in the cost of living, dockers' wages that in 1802 had been $5\frac{1}{2}d$. an hour never rose beyond this figure until by the titanic struggle of 1889—the strike for the Dockers' Tanner—they achieved the 6d. an hour than remained until 1911. From 1828 until the prosperous 1870s wages were steady at 4d.; an increase granted at about this time at the West India Docks to 5d. was accepted by the other companies. The few privileged men who worked at the Rum Quay, West India Docks, were, rightly, the highest paid of any and could earn 30s. a week. Similarly men who were prepared to work at Millwall Docks in the dusty conditions of bulk grain discharge, could earn as much as 9d. an hour as long as the work lasted. Many died before reaching fifty. Dealporters, another arduous calling, where men were too old at forty, could at the Surrey Commercial Docks earn a steady 30s. a week but only during the six months' timber season.

13

The dual control which followed the surrender of ship discharge and quay work at the lower docks ushered in so serious a change in port practice as to make necessary a description of the daily working life of the dockworkers. The broad picture is unlike that of any other industry. The detailed picture could not be bettered by a lunatic from Mars, given the mission of wrecking our ports. In varying this metaphor a French shipowner described it to me as an orchestra having different conductors for the strings, the wind and the percussion instruments and no agreement on the tune they were playing.

Commencing with the Tilbury and the Royal Docks the pattern here is of a large tonnage of goods in transit. At one time as high as eighty per cent, overside deliveries have now dropped in favour of road- and rail-borne traffic; tonnage carried by barge gets less each year. With its many hundred riverside wharves, its tributary rivers and canals taking barge traffic from the River Thames, the port of London shares with the complex of Rhine ports, the inestimable advantage of a healthy overside outlet. It is a fact, and ports from Rijeka to Keelung prove it, that a port whose only outlet is shorewards is inviting, and ensuring, congestion. The discharge of ships in the lower docks is in the hands of the shipping companies. They may themselves perform the operation through a stevedore department or they may employ a master stevedore to do the work for them. Whoever works on board will work also on the quay, receiving the cargo, taking it into the shed and delivering it, in the course of time, to road, rail or perhaps craft. The exception to this rule is bulk grain ships, the cargoes of which are handled at specialised installations equipped with suction elevators, also a berth where a steady import of bananas is discharged mechanically; both these operations are done by the PLA. To-bacco in hogsheads and casks is also warehoused here and there are refrigerated stores for frozen and chilled meat.

Exports at both groups of docks are received by the PLA, shedded by them and tendered to the ship as required. At this point, under plumb of the quay crane or the ship's gear, they are taken over by the loading stevedore, who may be the shipping company or the master stevedore they choose to employ.

The position at the East and West India Docks is more com-plicated.[1] In the 1890 agreement with the shipowners the Joint Committee insisted on retaining the discharge in the upper docks. They very rightly pointed out that whilst traffic in the lower docks was essentially transit by its nature, the discharge of cargoes at the India and London Docks was bound up with the busi-ness of warehousing—a main source of all dock companies' re-venue. As an example, until the Second War it was accepted practice for ships carrying cargoes of Cuban sugar, packed in three-hundredweight bags, to discharge directly into the ware-house sited immediately behind the transit shed and within a few yards of the berth on which the ship lay. The gangs making up sets of sugar in the ship's hold sent these ashore by crane or derrick; each set was landed on to a scale placed under plumb on the quay. As soon as the set had been weighed it was whipped off to an elec-tric truck and conveyed into the rear warehouse. Here fifty-ton piles of sugar were built and within a matter of days a cargo of some 10,000 tons of sugar would be piled and ready for sale on the London Terminal Sugar Market.

To make a through operation of this kind possible a single employer was essential and this principle was conceded by the shipping companies. In the West India Docks were also sheds, equipped with heavy duty overhead gantries, for piling hardwood logs, of which a stock of 50,000 tons was not uncommon. In the adjoining Millwall Docks there had been built a massive granary which, like those at the lower docks, discharged grain-carrying vessels by suction, stored the cargoes in the many-floored granary

[1] As the East India Dock has been disposed of (1968) as have also the London and St Katharine Docks (also 1968), ship discharge and loading problems will no longer arise there.

and delivered it, bagged if required, to road, rail or craft. To supplement the shore facilities that these granaries provided, the PLA, in its early years, took over at a cost of £80,104, from the London Grain Elevator Company, their fleet of elevators. The company had long enjoyed a monopoly of discharging grain from ships into craft, commencing with the early bucket elevators which had only a limited output. Needless to say, the Authority had increased the fleet and output now is limited only by the handicap of small craft, of an average capacity of 180 tons, that the port of London has persisted in using. In this respect it is at a disadvantage against the Rhine ports where a 3,000-ton barge can work uninterruptedly for a full working period without work stopping, whilst it is removed and replaced by an empty barge.

In considering the ways in which the various docks in London evolved and how the trend took a line different from that in the mind of the parent company, the problems of warehousing are of first importance. Dock developments in the nineteenth century ran parallel to a steady improvement in the standard of living. The wealthier classes demanded luxuries that could only be found in Africa, the Far East or America. Teas from China and (after 1840) from India and Ceylon, carpets from Persia and China, drugs and spices from the East Indies, rare hardwoods and fancy woods from tropical countries, all these poured into London, as the encroaching steamships made longer voyages economic. Parallel with the luxury trades the more staple imports grew apace. The cutting of softwood timber from the log dated from about 1820. The vast quantities of deals, boards and battens, as well as prepared imports such as doors, that were unloaded during the season at the Surrey Commercial Docks made possible the expansion of London from its eighteenth-century limits to the sprawling metropolis over which Queen Victoria ruled. Timber sheds by the dozen sprang up at both the Surrey Commercial and the Millwall Docks, while the West India Docks vied with them in the measuring and piling of hardwood boards and planks. At London Docks, twenty-six miles of vaults catered for wines and spirits from the Continent; at the West India Docks the Rum Quay a 'place of exceptional security', held some 20,000 hogsheads of Jamaica Rum. As a sideline, rum was vatted and bottled there to the merchants' requirements. Quite a substantial part of London

Docks was given over to wool, hides and skins. From Australia, South Africa and even the distant Falkland Islands, bales of wool by the thousand poured into the London and St Katharine Docks, there to be weighed, classified, sampled and put up in Public Sales. In the many warehouses in the upper docks merchandise from far and near, nutmegs, iron bottles of quicksilver, tin in ingots, ostrich feathers and indigo, to name only a few, found a secure home.

Security was in fact the keyword. Nearly all the goods mentioned were subject to duty. Only premises that can be made secure against thieves and fire will be approved by H.M. Customs for the temporary storage, in some cases for several years, of 'bonded' goods. Transit sheds do not come within this category. Therefore all goods that required storage in bonded premises had to be despatched, usually by craft, from the lower to the upper docks where suitable accommodation could be found. This is a very important aspect of dock work and it explains how docks such as the London and St Katharine, the East and West and the South West India Docks, also the Millwall Docks, were able to flourish for decades after ships had grown too large to pass through their entrances from the river. Behind the building of the Royal Albert Dock by the London and St Katharine Docks Company, in 1880, was the knowledge that much of the vast quantities of merchandise that would be brought into the new dock by the larger ships could be channelled into warehouses at Shadwell. The East and West India Docks Company, with similar intentions, embarked on its unfortunate building of Tilbury Docks a few years later.

This constant movement of valuable and highly dutiable cargoes from the lower to the upper docks has produced a well-organised lighterage industry that owns about 4,000 craft built on a design which stood up to the rough handling to be expected in the congested waters of the enclosed docks. With this has come also a specialised force of lightermen. The withdrawal of their labour has more than once brought the work of the port to a halt within days. They are a vital part of London port labour. To handle the incessant loading and unloading of barges is a major part of the work of the upper docks. A high proportion of the labour and staff there are engaged in warehousing work of which the unloading of goods from craft forms the first stage. The many

98

years of practice in dealing with special cargoes such as timber, wool, tobacco, wine and grain has produced little coteries of staff and labour that, throughout the years, has attained a knowledge of the nature of commodities and a skill in processing them to the merchants' requirements; a very tangible asset in attracting cargoes to the port of London. The gradual acquisition of this 'know how' has had, in one aspect, a deleterious effect on the port whose chief function many consider to be that of turning round ships quickly. Encouraged by mid-Victorian dock proprietors, merchants saw in the willing co-operation of dock staff and labour the means of preparing their imported cargoes so that they could be sold and delivered direct from the dock sheds. For example, fresh fruit was sorted and graded at the ship's side : importers were encouraged, in face of increasing competition from the wharves, to use the dock sheds as their own warehouses. Where the mercantile processes could be carried on away from the transit sheds, as with timber, wool and many other commodities, it was legitimate business and brought work to thousands of dockers. Unfortunately there grew up a tendency to give first place to merchants' requirements at the expense of ship turnround. It was often convenient for a merchant, with a rising market, to leave his cargo for weeks in a transit shed. During the congestion that followed the end of the First War, heavy Penal Rents had to be imposed to deter this abuse of shed space. With the coming of the larger cargo unit, to be dealt with later, the needs of the trade are taking second place to ship turnround.

To understand how dockwork, the main outlines of which have been briefly sketched, can, without difficulty, produce the material for disputes and stoppages, it is necessary to look at the division of responsibility that pervades the upper docks, as well as taking a look at the work done by, and the formation of, ship and quay gangs. To do this will show how unlikely a period of prolonged harmony can be. Although the right to discharge was maintained at the London and India Docks it has been eroded by the letting of dock premises to shipping companies who have introduced their own labour. At Millwall and the Surrey Docks the port authority's labour does no discharge or loading of general cargo ships. However, at Millwall Docks the curious arrangements still exist by which the PLA labour does the quay work, and this also applies to certain berths at the Surrey Commercial Docks. The port authority take over the cargo as it comes ashore and are responsible from then on for the transit and delivery work. With the exception of certain berths on long leases, all receiving of land-borne exports is done by the PLA who handle these through the sheds and, as required, tender them to the loading stevedores at the ship's side.

Lightermen have their own union and their industry is a closed shop. The tally clerks, whose numbers vary with the demand for their services, are a further essential part of the machine by which ships are discharged and loaded. Before a gang can start work on a ship it must be at full strength, as the system of the port demands; it must be headed by a ganger and contain two winch drivers or a quay crane driver. If cargo is to be landed, there must be an appropriately manned gang with adequate and suitable gear (electric or hand trucks), to take away the sets as they reach the quay. If the cargo is being taken overside then the barge belonging to the lighterage firm employed by the receiver of the cargo, complete with lighterman, must be placed in position alongside the hold containing the merchandise. A tally clerk employed by the shipping company or the master stevedore must be on the spot, ready to start work. He will tally the goods into the barge or ashore, as the case may be. If the latter he will, if the PLA are receiving the cargo, be tallying against their clerk.

If cargo is being loaded the same essential conditions apply in reverse. The tally clerk will record not only the number of packages loaded, either from craft or the quay, but will measure, for freight purposes, any cases that are not part of a homogeneous parcel. The ship's gangs, instead of making up sets of cargo in the holds, receive sets of cargo from the quay, break these up in the hold and stow each package safely and to the various destination ports. A medium-sized cargo ship may load at several ports both here and on the Continent and subsequently will discharge and perhaps reload at some dozen ports abroad.

The diagram reproduced illustrated the typical general cargo ship loading at South and East African ports and carrying cargo for the United Kingdom and near Continental ports. It has been over-simplified but was typical of conditions in the inter-war years. In the order of the holds, bales of wool in the 'tween decks, des-

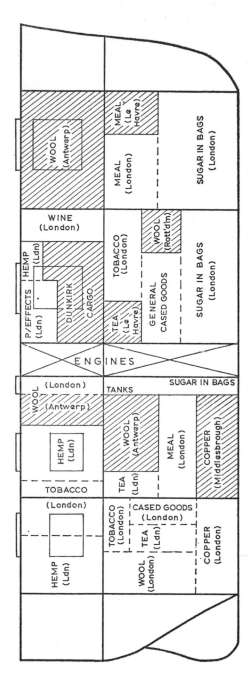

Cargo plan of M.V. *Molfetta*.

Cargo sent from South Africa to London, etc.

tined for Antwerp, will probably be delivered overside for re-shipping in a coastal-type vessel making the voyage to the near Continental ports. If it has been decided that the s.s. *Molfetta* will go to Antwerp—she may have cargo for South Africa to be loaded there—then sufficient of the wool to allow the discharging gang to make a trunkway to reach the London meal in the hold below, will have to be landed and reshipped later. The parcel of meal for Le Havre will be delivered to craft for reshipment, cer-tainly the sugar in bags will go overside to the receivers' craft for the refiners' riverside premises.

In No. 2 hold the personal effects and the wine will be landed, the latter requiring the attendance of a cooper qualified to sound out each cask before it is handled by the ship labour. Very likely the ship has called at Dunkirk on her way up the Channel and the Dunkirk cargo (wool in bales) will have been discharged. The parcel of hemp immediately below the top hatches will have to be delivered overside because hemp ranks as hazardous cargo and may not be put into a general cargo transit shed. If the receiver of the hemp has not got his barge alongside when the ship breaks bulk the port authority will supply a barge, known from sailing ship days as a 'Captain's Entry Craft', and the parcel will be taken to an approved hazardous goods store there to await delivery. The tea for Le Havre will go with the meal; also for this port the tobacco will probably go by barge to the PLA tobacco warehouses at the lower docks; the parcel of wool for Rotterdam will also be delivered overside; the general case goods will be landed and the sugar on the 'ceiling'—the floor of the ship—will go by barge to the refiners. The parcel of sugar in the tank accommodation will take longer to discharge than that in the open holds because of restricted working space and this must be allowed for in planning the working of the ship. Similarly cargo in Nos. 3 and 4 holds will be discharged overside or ashore.

The s.s. *Molfetta* carried, beside London cargo, goods for several Continental ports. This is known as 'optional' cargo. For the pay-ment of a small additional charge on the freight, shippers may exercise the option of deciding, between a prescribed group of ports, where they wish their goods to be discharged. This option has to be exercised very shortly after the ship breaks bulk. The original destinations shown on the ship's plan may, and very often have, been altered during the voyage or even during the discharge. This may present the officer responsible for turning the ship round by an agreed tide, with impossible conditions. I remember watching the last few bales of wool of a consignment of several thousand bales, being landed late in the afternoon. They were consigned to Antwerp and were to leave later by a succeeding ship of the same company. The discharging vessel was due to sail at 6 p.m.— it was going to be an easy finish. Without any warning to the dock, the City office of the shipping company decided to send the ship across to Antwerp. Someone there had the bright idea that she could take this large consignment of wool, now in the shed. The ship had two hours left to load this, a quite impossible task, and the berth was needed for a ship entering the dock during the night. Convinced that not even the PLA could work a miracle of this dimension, the shipping company reluctantly changed their plans but the incident is typical of the uncertainty that accompanied the handling of optional cargo. Until the ship had left the quay and it was too late to take out any more cargo or put any more back, one was never certain. When conditions allowed, optional cargo might be discharged direct into a 'feeder' ship, moored alongside the parent vessel, to the inconvenience of work in adjoining holds.

London is a tidal port. To lose a tide means holding the ship for twelve hours. If a ship that was discharged in London had been 'stemmed' for a drydock in Antwerp or Rotterdam, a delay of twelve hours could not be accepted. Passenger-cargo vessels run to a tight schedule. At the time of the ship's arrival in London, or even before, the shipping company will intimate the day and the tide on which they intend she should sail. The discharging officer responsible for producing the ship empty by that date has to take into account bad weather, labour and staff availability, conditions of congestion ashore and, possibly, craft shortage. If he considers that overtime should be worked during the early days of the discharge he will advise the shipping company who, of course, expect to get their ship without the expense of overtime working. The Second War, and the port conditions that followed its conclusion, made it impossible to insist on the stringent conditions that had been the accepted rule prior to 1939. I can say with some pride that while discharging ships as my regular work, from 1921 to 1937, I never missed a tide. To do so was the unforgivable sin; a sin that an officer with an eye to his career in the port did not commit. It was truly said that a discharging officer's working life was made up of just jogging quietly along from one crisis to the next. He needed more than his share of luck, and foresight, to survive.

14

Some space has been given to the pattern to be found in the routine work of the docks. It will have been worthwhile to have gone into some detail if only to prove that dock work is unlike that of any other industry, including agriculture. Also that a very great deal of organising ability is needed before the work can start at all. As well as all gangs needing to be up to strength for an early start barges must be there each with a lighterman in attendance; also the tally clerk must be there with his card and pencil at the ready. It must not be raining. If a gang begins to work cargo into a barge at 8 a.m. and the cargo runs out at 10 a.m. it is unable to turn over to landing other cargo because there is no quay gang available to take away the cargo. It may be that the emergency has been foreseen and the expense of the standing by of the quay gang for the first two hours has been accepted. Ships' plans were not always correct and discharge arrangements could be knocked for six.

It requires very little imagination to see from this by no means exaggerated picture of dock work that the patience of the men and also the executive staff, was sorely tried by conditions mainly outside their control. A dozen good reasons could be found each day for industrial trouble; some of these could have been prevented by a supply of goodwill that was not always there. The patience of the foreman shipworker and the foreman quayganger (the one directly responsible for the labour on the ship and the other for that on the quay) were severely tried in their daily struggle to maintain a semblance of harmony. It was probably the realisation that they shared their troubles in common. I remember receiving, after having a job to get the ship working smoothly after a 1 p.m. start, a telephoned order for thirty men to return at once to the North Quay, West India Docks, their home department, where a ship had unexpectedly turned up. It was common practice for ship men, temporarily unemployed, to be lent to an over-busy department in another dock; their arbitrary recall, often unavoidable, was a frequent source of friction and a handicap to the PLA, in competition with private stevedores. My foreman shipworker, a veteran of the South African war and an Old Contemptible, looked at the clerk with the order in his hand as though he would knock him down. Instead, he flung his book on the quay, tore off his cap, flung this on top of the book and then jumped on both of them. It was a perfect picture of a strong man in his wrath. 'It's not fair, it's not fair, it's enough to take the heart out of any man.' 'Well, Albert,' was all I could say, 'I hope you feel better now; we'd better go on board and try and sort things out,' which we did, not by any means for the last time. Although the Management were no doubt right in manipulating labour in this way it was very hard on the officer whom they expected to turn the ship round and to carry out their orders at the same time.

'The orderly confusion of ship discharge', a phrase beloved of the Victorian dock officer to describe his job, was not without meaning. To a visitor conditions on a busy discharging department were seemingly without a plan. Actually they were extremely well organised. Each man knew what his job was. He had done it many times before and he hoped to continue to do it. Anything in the way of change is anathema to the docker, even when the change is going to be to his advantage.

This brief review should include a few words about the specialist grades, the cornporters and the dealporters. The former were specialists in the handling of bulk grain and had, prior to the taking over by the PLA of the London Grain Elevator Company, worked exclusively for this private company. Their part of the industry is a closed shop, they have their own branch in the T & GWU, also their own delegate. The nature of the work each does provides plenty of causes for dispute and his job is no sinecure. The dealporters are dockers employed exclusively on handling softwood timber in the Surrey Commercial Docks, and for some years, to a lesser extent, in the Millwall Docks. The stevedores who discharge the timber vessels are not dealporters but the master stevedores who employ them specialise in this work. The many dealporters who sort, pile and deliver softwood are employed by the PLA. Whatever efforts the PLA, in the early years of its existence, made to break down the exclusiveness of these two grades, both repugnant to the dominant London and India Company, and whose influence was immensely greater than their numbers warranted, were unsuccessful. Cornporters and dealporters still work at their traditional trades. The importance of the latter has been much impaired by the mechanised handling of softwood but more so by the great increase in the importation of packaged timber which is, practically, general cargo. In the post-war decades more than one major stoppage has been directly attributable to the actions of the cornporters, allied to the intense loyalty of the general dockers.

Deliveries, part of the general cargo work, engage their own quota of labourers, mostly in the warehouses. The young and active men were attracted more by the rewarding job of ship work, with its opportunities of overtime working. As men grew older they gravitated to the steadier and less exacting work of the warehouses.

Until very recent times a major cause of friction has made itself continuously felt—the presence of the two unions whose members sometimes work together and at other times and places are completely distinct. The stevedores have always, and with some cause, claimed that their work was superior to that of the docker on the quay, the man pushing the hand truck. From Victorian days they were a potent force in dock politics. In 1919 they saw the need to ally their small union with the forces led by Bevin in his fight for the 2s. an hour. After the General Strike of 1926 a number of dockers from the T & GWU, the massive union that Bevin had built up in the early 1920s, seceded and offered their membership en bloc to the Stevedore Union. They wanted the voice of the docker to be heard through the action of a small and belligerent union, capably led, experienced, even in those days, in the art of brinksmanship. They were accepted by the Stevedore Union although they remained subservient to the stevedore element in what became known as the National Amalgamated Stevedores and Dockers Union. On account of the one-time colour of their membership cards, the T & GWU has always been known, even in the Press, as the 'whites' and the NAS & D as the 'blues'. Since 1945 the failure of the two unions to co-operate in the best interests of port labour has further embittered the inter-union relationship and has been a major cause in the unhappy history of post-war labour. They have steadily opposed decasualisation. Since 1967 when this was imposed there have been signs of growing amity that have made old dockers rub their eyes. These have led (February 1969) to a suggestion that old wounds be healed by a link-up of the Stevedores with the T & GWU.

It would be naive to regard it as an aspersion on dock labour that only by a system of money incentives will the maximum work of which the docker is capable be forthcoming. Piecework has been accepted as a fact for over one hundred years. A limited number of jobs were so performed in 1889. In the strike settlement the Joint Committee promised to increase this number.

Every part of the complex processes of loading, discharging and handling cargo is capable of being treated as an independent operation. What does the docker do for a living? *He spends all his life picking up and putting down again, generally one at a time, the myriad packages that make up the cargo of a general cargo ship.* Each time he puts a package down it should have been advanced one further stage in the long and costly journey from producer to consumer. The same principle applies to the warehousing of cargo; when a piece of timber is picked up from the landed pile, measured and then put down again in its final storage, it has gone one further stage towards its manufacture into a piece of furniture. Each operation (the making up of bags from a ship's hold and their landing on the quay, the removal of these by the quay gang and their piling in the shed, are two substantial examples) could, from very early days, be costed by the employer and a payment made to the gang. In theory, nothing could be more fair than such an agreement. In practice, few arrangements have been open to more chicanery and manipulation. The late Henry Ford I laid down two principles for piecework : you must first agree a fair rate and secondly pay whatever the men can earn on this rate. He added that, in his view, the best employer was the one that could contrive to pay the highest wages, the operative word being 'contrive'. The Joint Committee were prepared to reduce their costs by increasing the amount of work done directly for them on piecework, to the reduction of that hitherto done by contractors. They were apprehensive, with very good reason, of their ability to frame 'fair' piecework rates, i.e. rates that would be fair to the Joint Committee. They accepted the principle that the rate for the job (forty years later there were said to be over 40,000 scheduled piecework rates) when it was done by conscientious men, working diligently and secured from interruption, should produce for each man a payment equivalent to his time wages, plus one-third. On his post-strike wage of 6*d*. an hour the casual could expect to earn by piecework an additional 2*d*.

Having sanctioned an increase of $33\frac{1}{3}\%$ in the pay of many casuals the Joint Committee soon began to have doubts. Had they not been too generous—had they not been hoodwinked into accepting a basic tonnage that had purposely during the trial period been kept down by the men? Was it not a fact that some rates were regularly producing 3*d*. per hour surplus for a growing number of men, who prior to 1889 had been content with their 5*d*. an hour? Whilst creating an impression of much activity the men, they now alleged, were deliberately withholding their best effort. Now began a 'catch as catch can' period that lasted until the Second War and its later developments outdated the piecework basis for dock work. By keeping careful records the employer was able to show that, released from the trial period, men were earning over one hundred per cent on their basic wage. The rate was too high for the job and it must be reduced forthwith; in most cases it was cut down until the older men were unable to keep up the pace set by the younger and more active, and fell by the wayside. Others, more clever, went slow on rates hitherto outside the daily scrutiny. They were often able to force an increase on these. I remember being told, about 1930, by a Transport and General Workers Union delegate that in whatever gang he found himself working he made it his job to see that output was kept down so that a surplus of not more than the accepted one-third of the day-rate was earned. He admitted that, of course, he could work harder but it would only result in the rate being cut.

From its inception the system of piecework lay under a curse. Not always on the one side. Many discreditable practices were tolerated. With an amount of honesty and tact unlikely to be found on either side in the 1890s, it could have been built up into a simple system. The men would have been adequately rewarded and the Directors would have reduced their working costs. Instead, both sides seem to have accepted the challenge and blithely engaged in a struggle that can have only one ending—the taking over of the manually performed work by machine, a process that will later be described.

This is how a simple piecework bill is operated. The job to be done was the discharging into craft of sugar in bags; the period was around 1920 and the hourly rate of pay 2s. The rate for the job had been agreed at 11d. per ton, and the 'surplus' (colloquially known as 'plus') came out at the regulation one-third of the time-rate.

	£	s.	d.
Discharging overside sugar in bags. 300 tons at 11d. per ton	13	15	0
Guaranteed wages at 2s. per hour for 13 men working from 8 a.m. to 5 p.m.	10	8	0
Amount available for division among the gang	3	7	0
Equivalent to a payment of 7.7/10d. per hour surplus per man.			

From the above it could be concluded that the output of 300 tons represents the effort the men were prepared to make and a tonnage that would be acceptable to the employer. This is oversimplifying the position. No gang ever worked for a complete day and neglected the many opportunities, some legitimate, for boosting the bill. It may rain for twenty minutes during the morning; the ganger would enter this on his bill as '13 men standing by for rain, half an hour'. A winch may break down, a lighterman fail to have his craft under plumb at the required time. In any case in the discharge of 300 tons it would be necessary to take off a deck of beams and hatches. This would delay the gang for an alleged half-hour, which incidentally has come to be accepted as the minimum period for intermittent delays. It was the job of the ganger to see that no possible opportunity for boosting his daily bill was neglected. It was the job of the Authority's officer, from his personal observations, to see that these made some contact with the truth.

The most rewarding part of my daily duties as a ship discharging officer was spent with a blue pencil, cutting down the claims made for allowances on the previous day's bills. It was a game that both sides played according to the unwritten rules. On one occasion I thought that the other side were not observing these. A ganger had submitted a bill containing so many allowances that I was moved to add these up. They came to a total of $7\frac{1}{2}$ of the 8 working hours. In the remaining half-hour the gang asked me to believe that they had discharged 2,000 bags of meal, some 200 tons. This was the only part of the bill I could believe. I pointed out to the ganger that no day would be long enough to do all that he claimed to have done. I then tore the bill up and handed him the pieces. 'Now use your loaf,' I said, 'and make out a proper bill.' He grinned at me and accepted the fact that he had broken the rules.

Before leaving the subject of piecework I must emphasise the basis on which all piecework rests. It lies in the guarantee by the employer to pay, as a minimum take-home amount, the hourly rate agreed nationally, in this particular case 2s. per hour. Should conditions make piecework impossible, should the cargo be awkward to handle or should it rain all day, then the bill will be a 'niller' and the men earn no surplus, but receive their basic pay. With the years the principle of piecework became so embedded in men's minds that a job that could not be done on piecework conditions provided excuse enough for going slow. Piecework was a reward for effort, day work did not, according to labour, call for effort. This attitude was always mentioned as a reproach in the working of piecework ports; London has always been in this category. Until recent years Liverpool and other ports have always worked on a day-work system. As the system is assumed by the men to apply only to perfect conditions, which are seldom realisable, in practice every deviation from the perfect is considered as justifying an allowance for awkward or difficult conditions of working. This view, and it is the dominant one, is a prolific cause of dissension. Where men are looking for a dispute they do not have far to look.

The first attempt to settle the amount to be paid for interference with straight piecework is made between the local officer and the local delegate, or even the ganger. In the majority of cases a settlement of a kind that will permit the work to continue is reached. Should this not prove possible at the dock level it will next be considered by the Group Committee, composed of representatives of both sides. The cause of the dispute may involve an alleged breach, or a new interpretation, of a national agreement. The dispute that has started in the hold of a ship may be settled by the National Joint Committee who rarely fail to find a solution. This gives time for tempers to cool down and for the issue to become an academic one.

For overtime, officially deplored by the unions but eagerly sought after by the individual docker, payment varies for all-night, Sunday or Bank Holiday work. I have worked in the docks on every day of the year except Christmas Day which is, very rightly, sacrosanct. In the 1930s all-night working, continuous from 8 a.m. one morning until 7 a.m. the following day, was normal and was accepted as a useful supplement to the pay packet. Overtime conditions are complicated and it is only natural that the interpretation of the various agreements provided a fertile field for disputes.

One last word on working conditions, about 'take-home' pay. Knowing the thoughts of the docker on this most vital of subjects I was always amused at the management consultant and his productivity plans. As applied to the portworker they seemed to me to be based on the erroneous assumption that a docker comes to work to see how hard he can work and how much money he can earn. Nothing could be further from the truth. In the mind of every docker is the fixed sum he will be satisfied to earn and below which his domestic commitments will not permit his take-home money to fall. To secure this sum he will be prepared to work overtime nightly to 7 p.m. on those departments where it is customary. That he is, in effect, spreading eight hours' work over ten hours was made apparent in the late 1940s, when the blue union used the weapon of banning overtime. Within a few weeks sufficient tonnage was being handled in the shorter hours to ensure that the weekly pay packet, which included piecework earnings, contained the same amount as before the ban. The shipowners were the gainers.

As a daily example this is what used to happen. A ganger starting to discharge a hold containing bags of sugar at 8 a.m. noted that the day was fine, that there were plenty of craft and that the quality of his gang was good. An output of 350 tons would give each member of the gang 5d. surplus additional to the 7.7d. secured by an output of 300 tons. It was worth risking a cut in the piecework rate. 'What do you say to a shilling?' would be the way he would pose the problem of output and the gang would set to with a will. Herein lay a major snag for the inexperienced operator. In the inter-war years there was much kudos to be gained by young officers able to secure record outputs on ship discharge. I was once placed in this fortunate position. Apart from the kudos, I looked like winning a bet placed with a colleague if I could exceed 400 tons per gang during that day's discharge. To my delight I saw that the noon figures revealed an average of 250 tons. I congratulated the foreman shipworker on an output that must, by the end of the day, easily top the 400 tons. A veteran of dock work (he had worked on the *Cutty Sark* on the same berth), he explained with patience that I could scarcely be more ignorant of the docker and his methods. 'Don't you know, guv'nor, that the men settle what they are going to do before they start work? Today they have settled for 350 tons.' On my protesting that they had already discharged 250 of these he let me in on a truism that I have come to accept as basic dock knowledge and which, incidentally, won me a number of bets on wartime ship discharge in Italian ports. Without this knowledge no man should be permitted to express an opinion on dock work. The old chap was, in fact, restating the dictum of Dean Swift, two hundred years before. 'Two and two do not make four and the half of four is often five.' He went on to explain that the men had no intention of going home with a wet shirt. A man had promised his wife to take her to the Poplar Hippodrome that evening. It was only common sense that he shouldn't tire himself out when the morning was the right time to work hard. Kipling put it very well when he said : 'Morning never tries you till the afternoon.' As it was explained to me in 1925 it all sounded very elementary. Twenty years later the drivers of forklift trucks and mobile cranes used in the docks discovered that they had, without any intention, broken out of this hitherto unrelenting discipline. Machines do not get tired in the afternoon nor to any extent do their drivers. It became possible to expect an output in the latter hours of the day commensurate with the early morning hours. To see how this deviation from the accepted ways of working has influenced port productivity one can compare the trickle of general cargo discharged by a gang working during what was vividly and officially described as 'the dead hours of the night', with the output of the container ship whose owners, as well as the few men employed, regard day and night hours as being equally productive.

15

By the autumn of 1924 I began to look beyond the Wood Wharves
and to examine my prospects as an outdoor officer of the PLA.
I had learnt a lot about timber but I realised that there was a great
deal to learn about general ship discharge, the loading of exports
and the warehousing of general goods. About this time I came to
a conclusion, on which I acted; it ran thus : 'If you are comfortable in your job it means that you have learnt enough to know
all the answers. To remain longer in that department would be
wasting time and time is the most precious of all commodities.
Now is the time, therefore, to start further learning by going to a
strange and probably very uncomfortable department.' From this
one is led to understanding that trouble is not something to be
avoided at all costs, but a thing to be sought if, from it, experience
that will be valuable can be gained. Accepting responsibility gladly
follows naturally from this. For one man who will really do this
there are a dozen who will go out of their way to dodge it. When
the Second War came I found myself doing a job that was new
to the British Army : discharging vessels full of warlike stores. This
was work full of pitfalls for the Regular officer, but providing a
great deal of satisfaction to the officer who was prepared and
willing to stand on his own. In the event, and as from September
1939, it was conveyed to the higher ranks of the Army that one
knew not only how to discharge ships and how to run a port, but
that one did not welcome advice or control, from non-technical
officers, however senior. In the event also, many Area Comman-
ders, who knew that the port could quickly prove the trouble spot
in their command, were only too happy to leave this super Mec-

cano set to the Supplementary Reserve officers, making only occasional visits when things were quiet.

The part of the India and Millwall Docks that had the worst reputation as the graveyard of young and aspiring officers was the East India Dock. In 1924 it was the home of the Union Castle Steamship Company, Ellerman and Bucknall, Bullard King and Company and the Blue Star Line of meat ships from Argentina. Mainly concerned with the South African trade, both imports and exports, it had recently converted a general cargo berth to handling frozen and chilled meat. A berth not occupied by the regular users of the dock would be immediately snapped up for the discharge of a chartered tramp, with a cargo of sugar in bags, oranges in cases and, at times, a salvage cargo. There were still mines floating around and a salvage cargo meant pickings for dock labour and useful experience for the officer discharging her.

Hearing through the grapevine that the demotion of a third officer in four years at East India Dock was about to take place, I applied for a transfer. While Mr White was neutral the Dock Superintendent was not helpful. Knowing what a hot spot the East India Dock had always been he predicted for me either a wooden cross or, less likely, a Victoria Cross. From his tone he was not backing the latter for he added: 'And don't blame me afterwards.'

I arrived there on December 1st, 1924, to be greeted with no enthusiasm by a new Principal Warehousekeeper. This was understandable, for we were both 'new boys' and his experience, although much vaster than mine, had not included ship discharge, the prime occupation of the dock and one on which many junior officers had come to grief. Here I would remark that some of the good luck that has accompanied me all my life deserted me during the eight years I spent at East India Dock. I had indeed been fortunate during the early and impressionable years to have worked with a man of the calibre of Alf White. It was not required in those days that a dock officer should also be a gentleman, and very few were. For a long spell I worked under officers whose one aim was to stand well with the Head Office, even if this meant casting their junior officers to the wolves that prowled, without haste or rest, around the dock work. Shooting down Assistant Warehouse-keepers was a recognised sport for which there was no close season.

Right Rum Quay, West India Dock. Unloading a cask of rum from a barge, 1927.
Below No. 1 Warehouse, Rum Quay, on fire, April 1933. On the left of the crane jib is the bell tower from which men were summoned to work at 1 p.m. daily.

Left Floated timber— Surrey Commercial Docks. A rafter is scribing the name of the ship on a log. The method of keeping the raft together with head and breast ropes is clearly shown.

Below Sugar being piled in the open, under tarpaulins, on a bombed site. Additional protection given by sections of corrugated iron designed for the job, 1939-45.

The position was accepted by both parties—all dock officers were brought up to it. Consequently, it behoved every junior officer to keep a step or two ahead of the Principal, to anticipate his requirements and whenever it was possible (and this was not often) to allow him to fall into the pit that his ignorance and arrogance had dug. They were not happy working conditions; rather were they a challenge and I accepted them as being so. Every working day was a challenge. At the end of it, and some days lasted more than the twenty-four hours the calendar allotted them, you had to be able to say: 'I have come out on top; I have resisted the demands of the shipping companies, the lighterage and the railway people and, very important, those of our own people, to catch me out.' It followed that a move by a senior officer to protect the junior officers was not to be expected. Neither would one look to the Head Office to take your part against the complaint of a shipping company. In those days the customer was always right. Every little shipping and forwarding agent in the City knew that he had only to send in a complaint about the officer at the dock, for the Head Office to promise immediate satisfaction.

In later years, both as Traffic Superintendent and as a Superintendent it gave me a real pleasure to stand up against such evidence of this school of thought as had survived the Second War. A foreign shipping company whose vessels made use of my dock employed an English firm as their agents. It was a cut-throat business and the agent was understandably anxious that his Principals in Finland should be left with no doubt as to his zeal. He would write a letter to me on a minor mishap, such as the mobile canteen arriving ten minutes late, and would conclude with the veiled threat: 'A copy of this letter has been sent to our Principals in Helsinki.' When the form became recognisable I thought it was time that it should be stopped. I wrote to their Dock Principal: 'The Superintendent has received a number of letters from you recently drawing his attention to minor matters of dock working, on which you feel that you have grounds for complaint. Each letter has concluded by your informing him that a copy of your complaint has been sent to your Principals in Helsinki. Whilst the Superintendent recognises the zeal with which you attend to the business of the shipping company you serve, he feels that they would be equally impressed were you to send them, as heretofore the copy of your next complaint, refraining, at the same time, from sending him the original.'

Similarly, when the Head Office asked me for the name and explanation of one of my staff at fault, my answer was invariably that I had, as their Dock Superintendent, already dealt with the matter and there it ended.

Nothing that happened in my early days at East India Dock helped. The first ship on the part of the dock I controlled was a 'tramp' full of sugar and other bag and bale cargo from Australia. On the voyage she had made water in the forehold so that she was officially declared to be a salvage job. This usually meant a 'free for all', restricted only by such resistance as the underwriters could put up. It was a very good test for a young officer whose discharging knowledge was confined to a few log ships. However, the system built up over the years by the PLA and its predecessors was sound enough to carry an ignorant junior officer in its stride. The working of the ship, that is to say, the arranging of the gangs, both as to the number that could be employed and the men who composed them, was done by the foreman shipworker. He also arranged with the several lighterage companies when and at which holds their craft would be needed. He was, usually, the good friend of the ship's clerk, a senior tally clerk placed on board by the shipping company to control the detailed working of the cargo and generally to look after their interests.

In a similar capacity on the quay, reigned the foreman quay ganger. He had the unenviable job of 'meeting' the ship gangs as and when they landed cargo. As it was not always possible to predict in advance when this would take place, or for how long, he had to manipulate the labour, having regard, at the same time, to the demands of shed deliveries of cargo, both to vans and to craft. Labour that had not been successfully planned beforehand was therefore condemned to an unprofitable period of 'standing-by'; this was his direct responsibility. A good foreman quay ganger kept a few jobs up his sleeve for such emergencies. When labour was put out of work by an incorrect ship's plan or by the failure of the receiver's craft to present itself for cargo, this could be charged to the shipping company, who, naturally, would appreciate one finding alternative work for the gang. Weather was a factor over which the discharging office had little control. If the ship was in a hurry the practice had grown up of working a few hours' overtime, that is until 10 p.m. on the early nights of the discharge and when the weather was favourable. Of course, the shipping company did not like this and if the weather remained fair throughout the discharge they did not fail to tell one that they had been put to unnecessary expense. If the weather turned wet, and by having gained a few hundred tons by timely working, one was able to finish the ship in time for the appointed tide, nothing was said.

The experienced dock officer knew that his working life presented two chances: he could either be wrong or he could be incorrect.

In the 1920s, and, in fact, until the Second War, cargo consisted of small units of which only a minute number were too heavy to be manhandled. This system, one that had been accepted since the Phoenician galleys roamed the Mediterranean, was expensive of labour. Until the First War, labour had been the cheapest commodity in the docks. It was also very flexible. Men would make no objection to transferring from one hold to another or to working short handed until such time as the gang could be made up to strength. I have frequently ordered men who have finished a hold during a working period to finish that period by helping the gang on the quay. On one occasion I completed the discharge of a ship which left the berth at 2.30 p.m. It was replaced at 3.30 p.m. by an incoming ship of a different line. The gangs from the first ship stood by for an hour, and then began the discharge of the second ship. This meant that the owners of the first ship did not have to pay for standing by from 2.30 p.m. until the close of work at 5 p.m. Neither did the second ship have to pay for labour taken on at 1 p.m. standing by until it could make a start at 3.30 p.m. It was a sensible arrangement by which the shipping company and also the port authority benefited. Unfortunately, common sense of this order has now disappeared entirely from our ports.

Shortage of labour, vagaries of weather, delays to ships by fog, failure of craft to arrive on time or absence of rail wagons or tally clerks, these were the main but by no means all the causes of concern with which the officer in charge of the discharge had to cope.

The sudden news of a casualty to one of their freighters off the

African coast caused the Union Castle Mail SS Line to order the non-stop discharge of a sister ship, the *Cawdor Castle* that had just broken bulk; she was needed urgently to replace the damaged vessel and in the words of their Cargo Superintendent: 'The winches won't stop from now on.' She had some 6,000 tons of general cargo. My colleagues and I arranged to work her 'Box and Cox', and this included the intervening week-end. It meant that I would be in charge from 8 a.m. the next morning until I handed over to him at 7.30 a.m. on the morning after, thereafter taking turn and turn about. The same arrangements were made for staff and labour. The overtime pay was welcomed by all.

On the last night I had cleared the remainder of a parcel of sugar and successfully discharged some fifty tons of scrap metal, always an unknown quantity in ships' cargoes. Only a few tons of sugar remained on board and the Dockmaster had not asked for the ship until 10.30 a.m. Tired but satisfied, I met my colleague and the Cargo Superintendent on the quay and received their congratulations on a job which I thought had been well done.

Our complacency was rudely shattered. The ship's carpenter walked up to our little group and, touching his hat to the Cargo Superintendent, broke the news: 'I've just had a look down No. 3 —there's about 300 bags of sugar in the cupboard there in the 'tween deck.' To my surprise the Cargo Superintendent beamed on us. 'Well now, gentlemen, that explains what has been worrying me for the last two days—where she got that slight list from.' We were more concerned on how we were going to get the sugar out in time for the *Cawdor Castle* to sail on the tide. She was going to Middlesbrough and would be entered for port dues as 'empty'. If she took this cotchel of cargo on board she would be liable to full dues, a very expensive mistake.

The cupboard was in an awkward part of the ship; each bag had to be trucked out to the entrance door before sets could be made up. Fortunately for me there was no Continuity Rule in those days and I quickly snaffled a gang from a ship of the same line working alongside. Drawing on my goodwill with the Dock-master, I persuaded him to risk taking her out two hours after high water, for she was completely light when she finished. When I arrived home for what was left of my day's rest later that after-noon I realised that it was thirty-two hours since I had shut my front door. A long spell but one that excited little comment in those days.

After all these years I still retain a deep sense of gratitude to those invaluable pillars of the department, the foreman ship-worker and the foreman quay ganger. Being such strong characters they were frequently at loggerheads. As I walked into the shed the foreman quay ganger would accost me, throw up his hands and invite me to look at one of his gangs who had been held up for half an hour. Full of sympathy, I would go on board to find the ship's gang concerned struggling with an ill-fitting beam that had to be removed before the gang could get at the cargo in the hold below.

During the discharge of a cargo ship there are dozens of in-cidents that mar the smooth rhythm of the work. Sometimes they fall within the province of the ship and sometimes the quay. It is all part of the game that the ship should blame the quay and the quay the ship for delays that are not of their own making. It is part of the officer's duty to placate both as the occasion dictates. A good officer will come in time to regard his work as an extremely interesting game once he has mastered the rules. To be able to play the game to his own and his employers' satisfaction is an achieve-ment, particularly as the latter implies satisfying the many in-terests that use the docks.

A major irritant was, in the years before the Second War, the preponderance of 'optional' cargo to which I have already re-ferred. Last-minute decisions as to the destination of large parcels of wool, meal or copper could, and frequently did, wreck the plans that had been made for the ship to sail. Moreover, on these plans the berth had probably been engaged for a ship arriving on the same, or the tide immediately following that on which the occupying ship would depart. A decision made at the last minute to land more cargo, would, also, put the shed out of action for the landing of cargo from the next ship to arrive.

Exports, for which there were four and sometimes five berths in the East India Dock, worked to a more rational tempo. De-cisions to work all night could be anticipated by the tonnage of cargo already in the shed waiting to be shipped. Overtime was, in fact, the major interest that the staff felt for export ships; it provided a substantial fringe benefit to their salary or wages.

Normally an export ship would work continuously from Monday to Friday until 7 p.m. During the lean years of the Depression one shipping company decided that this was a racket that had gone on too long and promptly closed their ship down at 5 p.m. It has already been explained that the docker decides on the amount of his take-home money. Seeing this threatened, the gangs concerned decided that, deprived of 7 p.m. working, they would work until 6 p.m. on the Saturday, the closing day of the ship. This would give them week-end overtime rates, paid at enhanced prices, plus the hour at 'double-double' from 5 to 6 p.m. With the co-operation of the master stevedore who employed them, Saturday afternoon working became a regular and lucrative happening; it had little relation to the tonnage of cargo in the shed or in craft.

All-night working on exports was so regular with one Line that the work of the dock would have been penalised if the officer in charge had followed the rule for import working and remained on the job all night. It was quite common for import ships to work from 8 a.m. through till 7 a.m. the following day and this was in no ways regarded, as at other U.K. ports, as penal working. The staff concerned were given the next day off, a privilege that was most appreciated. Before the days of the telephone a foreman who had no reason overmuch to like his Principal was out for an afternoon's stroll after an 'all-night'. He found himself in the vicinity of his Principal's house. On impulse he knocked at the front door; he implored the mistress of the house to control her emotions for he had disquieting news of her husband who had fallen into the dock. Happily he had been pulled out and at this very moment the husband was sitting in the office boiler house, covered in a blanket and needing a complete suit of clothes, underwear and black boots. The foreman explained that he had volunteered to leave his work in order to get these.

A comprehensive outfit was soon put together, his return fare to the dock provided and the foreman, assuring the wife how pleased he had been to have helped, left the house. At his usual hour a perfectly dry husband arrived home in his normal clothes to be amazed at the warmth of his wife's welcome and to learn from her of his immersion in the dock. He heard also of the kindly action of the unidentified stranger who was heard subsequently complaining that he could only wear his new suit on Sundays.

To overcome the difficulty with export working, whose gangs had formed the habit of taking a combined tea and supper break from 8–11 p.m. it was decided that the officer in charge would satisfy himself that work had been properly resumed by both the ship and the quay gangs and then, not later than 11.30 p.m., he could leave the dock, taking care to be back not later than 7.30 a.m. the next morning. This was a very easy way of earning overtime but the period between 8 and 11 at night did certainly drag. Not until 1927, when the purchase of my first motor-car made it possible to come home at 8 p.m. and to return in some comfort at 11 p.m., was the problem of killing those three hours of unwanted leisure solved. When this procedure was repeated on the first three nights of the week (the line sailed their ships regularly on the a.m. tide on the Thursday morning), to leave work at the normal hour of 5 p.m. felt like having a half-day.

Nowadays staff of all grades would object to working such long hours and with such regularity. True, it did interfere with domestic life but money took precedence over comfort and one knew that there was a queue of officers from the non-overtime departments willing to step into one's shoes. Apart from the general work of the dock there was a fruitful source of overtime provided by the meat vessels at No. 1 berth. The working of these ships was controlled by the demands of the British housewife. The daily work all led up to the Sunday joint, provided by the discharge of the ship up to and including Friday, the peak day. Sunday working, which filled the butchers' shops on Tuesday, remains in my memory by an emergency over the men's pay that arose without notice one Sunday. In the office safe I had put the pay for some hundred and fifty men, sufficient for the morning's work ordered by the shipping company. At 11.30 a.m., following a demand for meat from the market, it was decided to work into the afternoon period. This meant that I should need, by the finishing time which might be any time during the afternoon, a sum of money equivalent to what I already had in the safe.

Where to get this on a Sunday morning? My chief I knew would be in church; he was not on the telephone and could not have helped me. 'Why not try old so and so?' said my ever-resourceful foreman, mentioning the name of the proprietor of a public house in the East India Dock Road. Off I set and on the suggestion of a complete stranger that he should, in return for my I O U, hand over some £300, almost the whole of his Saturday night's takings, he showed no concern and asked me what I would take while he fetched the money. The situation was saved and the money was paid back on the Monday morning when he could pay it into the bank. When I reported the incident to my Principal, instead of commendation I was reprimanded for going into licensed premises on the Sabbath. However, as he had no sensible suggestion to make on how to conjure a large sum of money out of the calm of a Sunday morning in the East End, I did not on a future occasion take the trouble to tell him. I have always found it to be a sound working principle never to ask permission from a senior officer for an act that he may rightly consider to be unorthodox. It is better to chance one's arm after being sure that there is a reasonable chance of success. After it has succeeded, let him take the credit for it, as the normal chief will not be slow to do. If it fails it is up to a man to talk himself out of it—in any case the senior will not know about it and will quickly disown any responsibility. I found this drill valuable in Army matters affecting port working.

Sunday work on meat ships was regular and predictable. In 1927 fifty-one Sundays were worked; the remaining Sunday was known as 'Black Sunday'. So much for the union's official deprecation of overtime. But nothing lasts long in dockland and this good time came to an end in 1928 with the return of the meat ships to Victoria Dock. Happily their place was soon taken by a newly formed company that imported naked stems of bananas from Jamaica. This was also perishable cargo working to a demanding market; to get the bananas on to this, overtime working was always required.

In addition to the urgent work of ship discharge and loading there was the continuous warehousing of hardwood timber, sugar and other commodities. As the volume of shipping fell during the years of the Depression (one ship from South Africa arrived with the derisory cargo of 300 tons) and permanent men were employed in increasing numbers in cleaning warehouse windows and other chores, I made a determined effort to turn the ample warehousing space at the dock into a home for timber. In this I was helped by the preference of the trade for an enclosed warehouse as against the open timber sheds at the East Wood Wharf and also because of new construction at the South West India Dock which was encroaching on White's territory. The permanent men at East India Dock, deprived of their traditional ship work, soon learnt new skills and adapted themselves to the slower tempo of timber measuring and piling. With ample space available we were also able to offer a few of the larger importers a concentration of their stocks in a particular range of warehouses. This was a temptation that few could resist. It was a real help when selling timber to be surrounded with their own stocks instead of having to locate their parcels over acres of storage space.

A constant import of unusual nature in those days, and one that required some ingenuity in handling, was the traffic of animals from East Africa for English zoos. It was a common sight for a vessel to arrive with a large canvas water tank rigged on her foredeck. When this was drained the discharging gang had the problem of slinging and lifting perhaps a dozen live turtles each weighing several hundred pounds. The dockers' 'know-how' solved this by laying an octagonal canvas cargo net alongside the reptile and then, with two men taking a grip of the far side of the shell, giving it a sharp cant that turned the turtle painlessly on its back. The loaded net could then be lowered safely into the waiting lorry on the quay, owned by a firm of soup makers who were known world wide. Late one night a ship of the Union Castle Mail SS Line arrived with a deck load of animals for which transport was already waiting on the dockside; one of the lifts consisted of a giraffe in a slatted wooden cage which enclosed the body but left the long neck protruding. We had him safely slung and on the way to the quay when the animal decided to sit down in his box. This completely shifted the centre of gravity, or as a seaman would call it, the metacentric point, but the presence of mind of the crane driver landed the struggling beast safely. Many years later at a meeting of the International Container Bureau, and during a discussion on the internal stowage of containers, I related this instance to show how the stability of a large container could be affected by the shifting of badly stowed cargo. An American shipper who was present neatly side-stepped the problem by remarking that, so far, no suggestion to carry live giraffes in containers was on the agenda.

My friends who knew nothing about the docks would often ask me about the unusual animals that I had handled from ships. Quite innocently, in a room full of people, I once brightly announced that I was expecting a baby elephant in a few days. A kindly interest was shown in my condition for some time after this.

16

In the inter-war years there was much tonnage afloat that was reminiscent of the earlier coffin ships. Bought during the Depression at rock-bottom prices (the Greeks specialised in second-hand ships that they were reputed to have bought for the ridiculous figure of £1 per ton deadweight), they arrived with only a few hours' notice at East India Dock with cargoes of sugar in bags, all for overside discharge. Mainly from Cuba, it was the heaviest and most inert cargo unit that the long-suffering docker had to handle. Sometimes it came from Australia in lighter bags but with the cargo settled into the stowage during the long voyage; the dockers called these bags 'tombstones' and they knew. Sugar from Mauritius was a slow and tedious cargo to discharge. The ships that carried these bags were loaded off-shore from native craft each of which held some twenty-five tons. As the sugar in each barge carried the grower's mark there could well be on a ship containing 5,000 tons some hundred or more marks, each of which had to be separately delivered to the importer's barge; 'barge drill' the dockers called it. A good turnround was difficult to get particularly as on many of these tramps the gear was defective. It was not uncommon for a derrick to come down; this was one of the hazards the dockers faced and one of the reasons why dock work has always been classed as a dangerous occupation. While we were glad to get the work that these ships provided it was little consolation to know their discharge had been turned down by master stevedores as decidedly unattractive jobs. 'Let the PLA have them' was a line that outside stevedores often took and told us so.

The basis of all piecework schedules is that cargo should be in clean and sound condition and this should apply also to the gear with which it is handled. That this was not always so was painfully obvious with salvage cargoes. Where water had entered the hold bag cargo was the first to suffer. What had left the loading port as a clean and well-stowed hold arrived as a sticky mess, offensive by its stench and hard to handle because the gunny bags had rotted. When the hatches were removed, the rate for the discharge had to be agreed with the men. The payments in excess of the normal rates had also to be agreed with the agents or the owner of the ship. They had to pay and had only the underwriters to fall back upon. It says much for our good relations that nearly always agreement was reached locally. This did not mean, and it was all part of the game, that an officer would not sometimes be caught out. In my experience I once agreed a payment of so much an hour while the job, a very difficult one, lasted. This taught me the meaning of the term, beloved of the docker, 'more days, more dollars'. It also earned me a well-merited rap from the shipping company. On the next occasion I refused the gang's demands, which I considered to be unreasonable. My Principal took the negotiations out of my hands. I waited in my office while he discussed them with the gang. At the end of an hour, during which time no work was done, he came into my office, picked up the telephone and triumphantly told the Dock Superintendent: 'I've settled the dispute, sir; we've reached a compromise and I've given the men what they've asked for.' I could hardly believe my ears until I saw his face fall and he muttered into the telephone, 'Oh sir, I never expected to hear you call me that,' as the Superintendent cut him off.

A good ganger was quick to pounce on any deviation from the normal as an excuse for an allowance to be added to his piecework bill. 'One man 16 hours—a bad plumb chafing my leg' was typical. In this case the ship had a slight list and the lowering of each set into the barge was thereby impeded by the set running down the side of the ship. How else would the ganger, a practical man, have expressed it?

I was fortunate, not in my principals, for none had the experience on which I could have drawn, but in the staff for whom I was responsible. My foreman shipworker was over sixty; he had worked in the East India Dock all his life. He was both trusted and respected by the shipping companies and by the gangers. An autocrat, he got his own way and he knew that his way was the right way. 'The *Cutty Sark* she was on this berth where we're sitting now, when I was a boy of twenty.' Famous ships like the *Thermopylae*, the tea clippers from China and the wool ships from Australia, he had worked on them all. Listening to him I learned some of the know-how of bygone days, some of it to come in useful later on. Similarly my foreman quayganger was a mine of useful knowledge although this was restricted to the quay and the shed. I learnt also that a good shed foreman could do things that were beyond my scope. At one time there was much trouble over damage to fresh fruit from South Africa, carried in cool stowage. Ten-pound boxes of grapes and peaches were particularly vulnerable. Walking towards the ship one morning I saw, to my horror, a set of these, some hundred boxes, on its way from the ship to the quay, foul a bollard and tip into the dock. The consequences were too awful for a young officer to contemplate. I turned tail and made for the barber's shop outside the dock where I had a leisurely haircut. Knowing that the music had eventually to be faced I made my way towards the ship. To my surprise, work was going on normally, nor could I see any of the chaos and confusion that I had pictured. Not being able to restrain my curiosity I said as casually as I could to my foreman : 'Oh, Tom, did you have a bit of a spill with some grapes earlier on?' 'Yes, guv'nor, we did,' he replied. 'There was a bit of a green-acre at No. 4 but I fixed it up with the runner,' mentioning the name of a well-known Covent Garden fruit merchant. That taught me that a shed foreman can do what an officer of the port authority would be foolish to attempt. Had I butted in the firm's runner would have made the incident official and a sizeable claim would have resulted. Working daily with the shed foreman he was not going to upset their mutually useful relationship over a few boxes of grapes. I found this principle to be important during the Second War. My soldier servant did many things to my advantage that I as a Lieutenant-Colonel would have been foolish to have tried.

In no way was this more vital than in the prevention of claims. The most contentious side of dockwork is, and always will be, tallying. No tally clerk approaches the ship's side with any intention other than to provide a count that will be favourable to his employer. If he is tallying for the ship then he will contrive to return the Bill of Lading quantity; if for the receiver, generally the PLA, then his tally will be agreed at a few packages short so as to provide for minor mishaps ashore. The whole system was, in the 1930s, a gigantic fiddle and all parties concerned in allotting or accepting responsibility for cargo whilst it was in their care entered into the game with zest. One firm of ship's supervisors went so far as to guarantee a ship's outturn before she entered dock. The facts and the truth were never wider apart. Particularly was this so with cargo that came directly off the ship, through the shed and into the waiting rail wagon or lorry. If your tally clerk had allowed himself to be bested at the ship's side—and there were a dozen ways in which the clerk tallying against him could do this—your shed foreman had to act quickly to prevent a sizeable claim. The Head Office did not like claims.

During the all-night working of a chilled meat ship in the bitter January of 1927, a tally clerk for the shipping company was the victim of what was regarded, when it later became known through the grapevine, as a perfectly legitimate move in the game. Knowing that he was likely to be two dozen quarters of meat short on the outturn my shed foreman gave his colleague, the foreman shipworker, the tip to have some extra sets made up and left in the wings of the hold. He would give him the word when to land them. Blowing on his cold hands he stopped to comment on the weather to his own clerk, who stood on the quay with his opposite number, the clerk protecting the interests of the shipping company.

'What about a mug of nice hot tea?' he asked the ship's clerk, who remembered his duty in time. 'What about my tally? I'd certainly like some hot tea.'

'That's all right, my bloke here will keep it for you, won't you?'

The PLA clerk, who knew how many beans made five, pointed out that this was strictly against regulations. However, seeing how cold it was and that the foreman was his friend, he didn't mind doing it for once. The ship's tally clerk was led away to a distant hut and handed a large mug of scalding tea. The foreman shipworker, who had watched the ploy from the ship's deck, landed six sets of meat during the ten minutes' absence of the ship's custodian. Two of these were duly recorded on the ship's tally card.

130

Potatoes from the Mediterranean were at one time shipped in native-made wicker crates, the tops being covered with gunny sewn to the wickerwork with twine. Knowing that he was two crates short of a parcel just landed, my foreman had his own idea on how this could be adjusted and a claim avoided. Taking with him an empty crate of the correct kind, he proceeded to 'bleed' each full crate. Lifting the gunny he was able, by poking in two fingers, to extract a potato at a time from each full crate, leaving the ullaged crate apparently sound. The job was going well and he had almost filled the first of his spare crates when a voice behind him demanded :

'And what are you doing to my potatoes?'

Getting up from the shed floor, he recognised the owner of the cargo he was broaching.

'Good morning, sir,' he replied cheerfully. 'I'm glad you've come down to the dock. I was down the ship's hold just now and I saw some loose potatoes lying about so I collected them in this crate. I've been stuffing in a few here and there where I found I could push them under the gunny.'

The importer, who was paid on the delivered weight of his crates, beamed on the foreman, gave him a pound note for the trouble he was taking and said how glad he was to see his interests so well looked after. Having seen him safely out of the shed the foreman was able to complete the job without further interruption.

Certainly of more importance in getting the work done was the ability of the officer responsible to secure the best of the labour. The three officers then working in the East India Dock were supposed to reach agreement on a fair share of the available labour. Demand varied from day to day; the work they were required to do varied from the discharge of meat to timber. There was, in the earlier years, a chronic shortage of labour. This was made up by calling on 'B' men. When those in the departmental lists of the dock had been exhausted, 'B' men, if they showed up from other docks, were called. The muster at 7.45 each morning was a scramble, and the wise officer made a point of attending this in person to ensure that he had, not a fair deal, but all he wanted for his work. To get the right type of labour for a ship due on the next tide was a problem, failure to solve which meant delays and frustration on her discharge. I came to recognise, watching the mistakes made by other officers, that the hardest part of ship discharge was done before the ship arrived. Nowadays it would be called 'planning in depth' and a computer brought in to help. Then, if anybody gave it a thought, they would dismiss it by the remark : 'He knows how many beans make five,' a high compliment in the dockers' world. Not for nothing have ships always been feminine. They are temperamental even in port. An experienced officer can tell a hundred yards away from a ship that the discharge is going well; she is, in fact, a 'happy' ship. Similarly, a ship that has a bad start, through insufficient preparation, will drag all the weary length of her discharge. Lightermen and other users of the dock are keen critics of all that goes on there and their approval is worth having.

The selection of the operating staff is another important matter that has a direct effect on labour performance. Like the dockers, some are better than others. As a young officer, I learnt how fundamental to success it was, firstly, to pick out the right man for the job, and secondly, having given him my full confidence, to leave him alone to do it.[1] In the 1920s there was on the silent films a strip character named Felix. He was a masterful cat that walked about with his hands behind his back. Before the time came for me to leave the East India Dock I learned that I had early been given the nickname of Felix. I was flattered at this because to have been accorded a nickname meant, in the Victorian phrase, that you were 'a man with a name about the place'.

In April 1926 we became aware that the growing industrial unrest which had stemmed from the long-standing disputes over miners' working conditions might affect the dockers. The idea of a General Strike where all work, including the docks, would cease was a new one. Despite the fact that since the Shaw Award there had been few labour disputes in the docks, all work stopped on the morning of May 4th, 1926. Maintenance work in the lock entrances followed a few days later. A government appeal, quickly answered, for volunteer dock labour produced for the East India Dock some 150 eager but inexperienced helpers, but included a few stevedores from the outside wharves who played a gallant

[1] Lord Sanderson, the late Chairman of Shaw, Savill & Albion Shipping Company and a prominent figure in the shipping world, in his Memoirs *Ships and Sealing Wax*, published in 1968, pays tribute to this same principle which he adopted in the shipping world.

Above Dockers in No. 2
Docks Group R.E. in
training at Longmoor,
August, 1938.
Right C.O. 5 Docks
Group R.E., England,
1943.

Above   Canadian cold store, Surrey Commercial Docks during fire blitz, 1940.
Below   West India Dock—part of the eleven warehouses built for the storage of sugar in 1802, after enemy bombing in 1940.

part in getting the work going. I mention this as an example of the contrary thinking that one constantly meets in the docks. Having shown their loyalty to the union, and their sympathy with the miners, by leaving their work at the wharves, they felt it their duty to help the Old Country by joining the volunteer force working in the nearby docks.

The story of the General Strike, except as it affected dock labour, does not come into this account. It is sufficient to say that all our dock labour, and all our staff, save a few of the senior clerks, left work. On the day preceding the total stoppage I asked several of the men why they would be withdrawing their labour. They were very glum over the whole situation; they could give me no specific reason and mumbled about loyalty to the union and such-like. Unemployment was general and steady jobs were not to be had for the asking. I think they were all glad to come back to work on May 17th with only the loss of their pay. There was, in the agreement made by the employers prior to re-engaging the permanent men, provision made for as many of the volunteers as wished to remain as permanent dockers. This followed the precedent of the 1889 strike. Fortunately tempers were, in 1926, very different. Very few volunteers elected to remain and certainly none in our dock. As we interpreted it on our local level the general spirit was to forgive and forget. On neither side was any reference made to the unfortunate aberration on the part of labour. In higher quarters, and also in the Royal Docks, the strike left an aftermath of distrust and resentment. A very small number of the staff were suspended for a few days; their prospects of promotion, looking back over the years, do not seem to have been impaired.

The country generally was now approaching the dreary years of the Depression. Under-employment made itself felt soon after the General Strike. Our particular barometer was our 'B' List. The rate at which these supplementary dockers were engaged, the number of attendances they were called on to make in each quarter, was an undeniable proof of the state of international trade. With the Wall Street crash of 1929 things got rapidly worse. This was no seasonal recession nor a temporary trade slump. It had to be recognised as the drab pattern for the foreseeable future. Whilst the PLA could do nothing for their 'B' men, and no permanent labourers had been appointed from this source since 1922, they worked out a scheme which did much to spread the load among their permanent dockers. There were already far too many of these for the work offering, as the 1920s drew to a close. Temporary expedients such as inducing men to take a day or more leave (unpaid), the cleaning of warehouse windows and other unproductive domestic jobs were palliatives only.

The scheme became known as the 'Stand-off'. According to the surplus permanent labour over the whole port, each dock was allocated its proportion of men who would be required to stand off on the following day. This stand-off was done in strict rotation and it fell equally on the highly specialised labourers as on the ordinary truckmen. It was not only fair but it was seen to be fair. It was the alternative to a wholesale dismissal of the men who had worked in the docks for years and whose chances of employment outside would have been slight. As trade improved by the middle of the 1930s the scheme was pushed into the background. Officially it remained and could have been reinstated until abolished in 1947 by the introduction of a new form of agreement between the authority and their permanent men.

The climate in the decade preceding the Second War was favourable to discussion and compromise. There was everywhere what was later described as 'a healthy element of unemployment'; certainly labour was in a more reasonable state of mind than that of the ten years immediately following the First War. Progress was made in the working out of a practical conciliation machinery. A system of Joint Committees operated to consider disputes which resisted settlement at local levels. If trouble arose locally and could have spread, an immediate meeting of our Joint Committee was called and there was some very plain speaking if agreements had been broken. The system was successful because it recognised and dealt with one of the main causes of trouble in the docks. If a gang think they have a grievance over piecework rates or conditions they make immediate representations to the local officer. If a settlement is not within his powers he will refer the problem to his Dock Superintendent. Failing agreement at this level the dispute goes to the labour specialist at the Head Office. As he is also Secretary of the PLA Joint Committee he can, after weighing up the threat to the work involved and after discussing it with the union representative, call a meeting of the Joint Committee, often on the same day as the trouble brew up. By this means a decision is reached and a minor dispute does not develop into a major stoppage. The point was brought home to me at the end of the Second War. A Company Sergeant-Major, an expert stevedore from a London wharf, while talking to me about his return to London's dockland, told me of his forebodings about the conditions he would meet there. As he remarked, any problem over ship working in the wartime ports could be referred to the OC of his company, a decision would be forthcoming, and this would be accepted. 'When I get back to civvy street,' he said, 'and I put anything up, it will take weeks to go up and up and then down and down. The odds are that by then I shall have half forgotten what it was all about—or more likely, trouble will have flared up.' Granted that conditions in civil life present more difficulties than those governed by military law, the fact stands out that a system that will produce immediate decisions is a good one. The London Shipowners had machinery of the same kind which worked effectively. They had also, in line with the Authority, produced a revision of the pre-1914 piecework schedule more in keeping with post-war conditions. These had been going ahead to the steady accompaniment of improved quay cranes and ships' gear. The electric quay crane first used in the docks at the turn of the century had been more efficient and was gradually replacing the hydraulic crane, itself subject to many improvements over the Victorian 'Coffee Pot'. Ships' winches were moving over to the electric roundabout deck crane whose driver did the work of two winchmen. These might well be called the harbingers of a mechanical spring. With the electric truck used first on meat cargoes in 1922, the mould into which all cargo handling had set all through the nineteenth century was beginning to crack. Not realised by port operators at the time, the way was being prepared for the wholesale mechanisation of the late 1940s. In the years immediately before the Second War there was general satisfaction at the way we got through the work in the docks that the rearmament programme brought. Labour worked well, the supervision was good and tonnage per gang hour, the criterion of cargo handling, was constantly rising. It took a major war and a thorough

135

bombing of our ports before we were able to take a new look at dock work.

The poor relations that had existed between the two unions since the secession of a block of docker members from the T & GWU after the General Strike became steadily worse after the Second War, and this had a bad effect on labour matters. Only in 1967, with the final decasualisation of dock labour and the threat of wholesale redundancy that could no longer be ignored, did peace break out and it became possible to give a meaning to 'Dear Brother' and 'Yours Fraternally' which had persisted in inter-union correspondence during the thirty years of active feuding. In 1968 they had got so far as appointing a joint committee to negotiate with the employers, a very sensible step. Wholesale redundancy, with its diminishing union membership, is a threat hanging over the heads of the unions as well as over those of the members.

In 1932 I left the East India Dock and went back to the Wood Wharves. White was about to retire and his deputy was demanding general experience and the chance to earn some overtime. It fitted into the management's plans that I should go back to the Wood Wharves, like a modern Aaron to stay the hand of a new Moses. The great days of the East India Dock were over. The inter-war tendency to build larger ships drove our familiar lines to the Royal Docks. The meat ships had left us in 1928; trade had not recovered and we were still in the Depression. My place was not filled.

I have given this picture of the East India Dock in the years between the wars because it was typical of conditions in the port generally. It was not a period of expansion. There were enough berths for the ships that offered. A major port improvement replaced the out-of-date jetties in the Royal Victoria Dock by a new lineal quay equipped with excellent warehouses, but no new dock was built during this period. The East India Dock had been a lively and active place where work was as likely to be going on during the night as during the day, or the week-end as during the normal day. For the officer the fear of losing his job, or even demotion, was never absent. That this was kept in the background is proved by my recollection of these years as both happy and formative for a young officer. It was there that I mastered the fundamentals of command as well as the basic groundwork of my trade. There was, despite the daily struggle for power that never ceased, a mutual respect and liking between the shipping companies, the Authority's officers and the labour and staff. We had learnt to get on with each other during many wet all-nights, we had learnt to rely on each other during the many crises that dogged the footsteps of an officer. It was a valuable training for the military command that was, unknown at the time, so soon to follow. Perhaps I can sum up the relationship by putting it in the form that expresses the grudging liking of the front-line soldier for his company commander: 'He's a bastard, but he's a fair one.' No dock officer is likely to get higher praise than this.

The next five years at the Wood Wharves were not exciting. After the East India Dock I found the limited tonnage, handled by a small but proficient staff, and the regular hours of working, monotonous. During my eight years' absence, the department had absorbed the Rum Quay that had hitherto separated the East from the West Wood Wharf. The latter was, in 1933, demolished to make room for a modern quay and warehouse let to a Norwegian shipping line who were allowed, and this was a precedent in the India Docks, to do their own work. A welcome addition was the transfer of the stocks of floated timber from the Surrey Commercial Docks where major improvements were taking place, and which addition had been welcomed by Mr White. Large tonnages of rafted pitch and Oregon pine logs were handled by half a dozen staff rafters who got on quietly with the job of receiving their cargo from ships that discharged in the West India Docks, ponding, rafting and measuring this cargo. It was a skilled and remunerative part of the business, had never been known to produce a labour dispute and on which the supervision required was at a minimum. It did, however, interest me that timber of this kind and in this form was still handled as it had been 3,000 years ago.

Faced with the problem of getting timber of a suitable kind and dimensions for the building of his Temple in Jerusalem, King Solomon turned to the only timber resources of the Middle East, the Cedars of Lebanon. His father, King David, had earlier received sufficient to build a royal residence. When, many years later, I saw the remnant of the huge forests that covered the Lebanon, I could appreciate how valuable this timber must have been in a land which was devoid of marketable timber in any other form. No wonder the few remaining trees are now many miles from the coast and are commercially inaccessible. The words in the account of this transaction by which Solomon procured timber are worth quoting (1 Kings, v). To Hiram, King of Tyre ('for Hiram was ever a lover of David'), he said : 'Now therefore command thou that they hew me cedar trees out of Lebanon.' And Hiram sent to Solomon, saying, 'I will do all thy desire concerning timbers of cedar and fir. *My servants shall bring them down from Lebanon into the sea and I will convey them by sea, in floats* unto the place that thou shalt appoint me . . . and will cause them to be discharged there . . . and thou shalt receive them.' The version in 2 Chronicles, 11 is more specific : 'We will bring them to thee in flotes, *by sea to Joppa and thou shalt carry it to Jerusalem.*' The Lebanon rafter of 3,000 years ago could have taken his place in the West India Docks with the rafters of 1932. Hiram, being a business man, made an exemplary C.I.F. contract with his customer, Solomon.

Although it had little effect at the time on the departmental labour, the burning down of half the Rum Quay in 1933 did quite a lot to clear the ground for modernised berths. When the remainder of the early nineteenth-century storage space for rum was destroyed by Hitler's blitz, room was made for a modern quay and two ultra-modern warehouses, embodying transit sheds and the latest ideas for mechanical handling of cargo. Like the General Strike, this event, which had been anticipated as something, were it ever to happen, that would destroy half London, was controlled without difficulty by some sixty-five fire engines and 360 firemen. Sentimentally it was a loss. Dickensian in structure (the gallery protecting the quay had been salvaged from the Great Exhibition of 1851—the other half was incorporated in the approach to the railway station at Crystal Palace, it was equally old-fashioned in its working methods and equipment. The very attractive cargo handled there had made it necessary, at the time of its building, to protect the land side with a deep ditch and either end with heavy iron fireproof doors.

Rum, distilled from the juice of the sugar cane, is imported at a strength adjudged to be unsuitable for human consumption. Until it reaches a proof strength of about 125 degrees it remains a potable spirit but it cannot be sold retail at a strength of more than

75 degrees. Reducing the potency of the spirit was done by vatting, when water was added. Rum can be an attractive drink around 100 degrees.

It has the useful quality of destroying germs; it will preserve a cadaver, whether human or not. 'Nelson's Blood', the name by which it has been colloquially known since Trafalgar, has a factual basis. After the victory Captain Hardy was faced with the problem of bringing the body of his dead friend, and the nation's hero, back to England. The only resources available off a hostile coast were the skill of his coopers and the Navy's stocks of rum held for issue to the crews, depleted in the recent battle. Enough rum was collected to fill a specially made cask into which the body of the dead admiral was reverently placed. After a long and tedious voyage the *Victory* arrived at Portsmouth and the corpse was handed over to the Admiralty, in a fit condition for the lying in state.

My Vaultkeeper, who loved this story, was proud of his throw-away line: 'And you don't think they poured the rum down the drain afterwards, do you?' According to the version of Thomas Hardy, the poet, there was none left by the time that Portsmouth was reached; I think that this is the more likely.

One recollection I shall always keep. In the Vatting Floor, where vatting, bottling and labelling were carried out, stood a monster vat holding 17,000 gallons. A very old and long-pensioned cooper enjoyed visiting his former department and the day was made for him when he could persuade a newcomer to walk with him to the Vatting Floor. Standing in front of the enormous vat, with an embracing sweep of his arm he would say his piece.

'Do you see that, my boy?—17,000 gallons it holds.'

Leaning confidentially over his victim he would add, impressively: 'I've drunk that in my time, I have.' Whether his arithmetic was correct, and I have no reason to doubt it, he continued hale and hearty well into his nineties.

Although in time I mastered the dockers' argot, I give pride of place to that which was peculiar to the Rum Quay. To me, pure *Alice in Wonderland*, I was not alone in suspecting it to have been deliberately contrived to 'fox' the layman. The 'contents' of a cask defined its capacity when empty, the 'ullage' the number of gallons when full, the 'wet' the dry part between the level of the rum and the underpart of the 'shive', as a cooper called the 'bung'. One term, 'Pompey', defied elucidation. This was the name given to the temporary head placed over a newly made cask when, to tighten its component staves, it was placed over a slow fire made of oak shavings from the staves.

I thought that it had a naval connection, probably with the eighteenth-century Admiral Vernon, who first watered the Navy rum and after whose grogram cloak the devalued liquor was named. I put the question to a veteran cooper on the department. The old boy carefully laid his hammer and chisel on the head of the cask whose hoops he was driving, and pushed back the little 'Fifth Form at St Dominics' cap that he habitually wore.

'Pompey—of course I know where it comes from. If I were to tell you that, sir, you'd be doing my job inside of a week.'

In 1937, having by now learnt all the answers, I applied for and obtained the job of investigator in the Department of the Dock and Traffic Manager. This time it was to the magnificent building on Tower Hill, the pride and joy of its architect, Sir Edwin Cooper, that I went. I left the placid millpond of the Wood Wharves and plunged into the crowded traffic of a busy river.

I arrived at a time when several changes had been made in the management, following on the retirement of many of the remaining senior members of the dock companies staff. In its earlier years the PLA, very naturally, preserved the outlook and the traditions of its component companies. These continued to be bounded by the dock fences. The modern conception of a port authority, the responsibilities it should accept for the port as a whole and the lead that it should give to shipping that uses the port, had to wait on the disappearance of the Moguls who conceived their duties only as being good landlords. New men came in from outside, a few of our own contemporaries had scaled the ladder of promotion more quickly; it was in the latter particularly that we placed our hopes for the future. Among these men of promise was Mr (later Sir Robert) Letch,[1] who had risen from being my contemporary in the Charges Department in the Leadenhall Street office in 1921, to the responsible position of co-ordinating the work of the five Dock Superintendents. He regarded this remit as including the bringing up to date of the many

[1] Died in 1963 as Chairman of the British Transport Dock Board.

activities of the port that had always been jealously guarded by the shipowners and the wharfingers. I became one of his three Investigators; dominating his department were the methods he had brought with him. He was a perfectionist. If one was not able to reach and hold the high standard Letch set, one was, after being somewhat roughly handled, quietly dropped. One took very little further part in what he rightly thought to be the exciting game of modernising the port of London. Several of the staff had already been weighed in the balance; on being found wanting they were allowed to continue with their limited activities, whilst they waited hopefully for the time when a less exacting successor allowed them to revert to the homely routine in which they had been reared. Although this certainly sorted out the good from the less good, it meant that the work of a busy department was done by the three Investigators and a few of the clerks who had measured up to Robert Letch's standard.

He was not married; the domestic life of his favoured staff took up less of their time as his demands on them grew. Typically, he handed me a 'sticky' job at 1 p.m. on a Saturday, remarking that he would have a chat about the matter on Monday morning. 'Don't spend too much time on it, old chap,' he added, one of his more engaging features being an illusion that he was considerate to his staff. I knew only too well that I had better know the matter in all its aspects, and possible repercussions, by 9 a.m. on Monday. Typical of his methods was his treatment of the Factories Act of 1937. This was a complex Act which impinged on working conditions in the docks, hitherto regulated by a Statutory Rule and Order issued by the Home Office in 1934. The eighty-odd paragraphs of this pamphlet constituted the dock officer's bible. They were taken so seriously that the Factories Inspector, known throughout the docks as 'Charlie Hatches', from his obsession with bolts in the hatch beams, could not come into the dock without his arrival being telephoned to every department and shipping office. How would this massive new legislation, by amplifying, correcting or cancelling, affect the existing docks' regulations? The clerk who dealt with safe working in the docks had only one idea and that was to send a copy of the new Act to every Dock Superintendent. Three out of five of the then Superintendents would have placed his initials on the cover and thrown it into his 'out' tray. The remaining two would, to their credit, have made some effort to read the Act but with little practical results. The construction put by Letch on the situation consisted of handing the whole job to me, to pass each of the existing docks regulations through the Act, to discuss legal points with the Authority's solicitor and practical points of gear with the Chief Engineer. If I thought that any of the other principal officers should be brought into the discussions I had a free hand to do so. He intended to issue a directive to the docks, setting out how they should act, when the conditions of the Factories Act of 1937 came into operation. That we were able to do this, and the directive consisted of only one foolscap page, was a personal triumph that taught me a lot. I learnt to read and to study small print; a valuable accomplishment that few people take the trouble to acquire. Having thankfully put the papers away I turned to the more engaging task of overhauling the ship-men arrangements at the West India Docks, only to find that I had, willy-nilly, become the Authority's expert on safe working conditions overnight. Almost immediately the major issue of warehouse loopholes for cargo deliveries was raised by the Home Office. Many of our older warehouses were never likely to comply with the new conditions; buildings at many of the wharves were even worse. The knowledge that I had gained from my recent study of the Act, plus the practical conditions in the docks on which I could speak with authority, won the day for the PLA. It was estimated by the Chief Engineer that it would have cost us £50,000 to have put our premises into the order demanded by the Home Office.

After that experience I accepted the burden of expertise. I found the knowledge valuable when working ports abroad for the Army. The Navy, supreme as they were in the Mediterranean, had no answer when the appropriate section of the Factories Act was thrown at them. I had hardly returned to the PLA when, early in 1946, the Factory Inspector became active once more.

'Let me see,' said a Dock Superintendent through the telephone one day, 'I seem to remember that you were the expert on safe working before the war. I've had the Factory bloke to see me and he's trying to tell me that our cooperage shops in the tobacco warehouses are factories within the meaning of the Act. I don't know what he's talking about so I've told him to come and see you.' It taught me that the reward is there if only one will take the trouble to master a subject that is unattractive to the majority. It also enabled me as a Dock Superintendent to snap my fingers at the Home Office when they tried to impose restrictions on the traffic in my dock.

My work under Letch's direction took two distinct lines for each of which my training was useful. One was to improve our ship discharge at the West India Docks. Unhampered by the restrictions on the employment of labour which hindered the Authority's officers, several of the up-and-coming master stevedores were taking work from the PLA. The 'B' lists on the discharging departments were my first objectives. They had not been revised for years beyond the minor changes made departmentally each quarter. By scrutinising the attendance records it was possible to prune these lists of men whose names, often for sentimental reasons, had remained too long on the lists for any value that their work still held. Many had found other employment. When the rationalisation of these lists had been done, and numbers reallocated to meet modern needs, there was a distinct improvement in our gang-hour figures.

The second job was to bring up to date the handling of hardwood timber. Here there was limited scope and very considerable opposition from the trade. They were not concerned that the increasingly retail nature of the teak trade in particular had made the storage, by the Authority, of this commodity completely uneconomic. However, by enlisting the interest of, mainly, the junior officers on the timber departments, we did receive some useful suggestions, many of which we were acting upon when the Second War put an end to a traffic that was never again to resume the prominent position it had occupied for so many years.

Relations between the port employers and the three unions representing dock labour (the third was the Municipal and General Workers Union who rarely intruded on negotiations) were improving gradually as the memory of the General Strike faded. There was much general sympathy with the privations that the Depression had brought; there was also a genuine appreciation by labour of the humane application of the stand-off scheme as an alternative to dismissals. There was a general feeling that the time was ripe for re-opening the problems of decasualisation. The

144

opportunity came in 1937 when Ernest Bevin made a demand to raise the daily rate of pay, which then stood at 12s. a day, to 14s. To have granted this rise would have improved the dockers' take-home pay but it would have done nothing to help solve what every far-sighted employer knew to be the real problem—decasualisation. When the suggestion was made of an immediate rise in pay to 13s. and a promise to tackle the administrative difficulties of decasualisation, the unions accepted the compromise. 'Work or maintenance' had run like a thread through every negotiation since the report of Lord Shaw in 1920. It remained right through the various forms taken by the Registration Scheme administered by the National Dock Labour Board from 1941 onwards, until in September 1967, nearly twenty years after Bevin's death, it became a reality. A fillip to the early discussions was the suggestion that the government of Mr Baldwin should show their sympathy in a practical form by partly financing the scheme with the £1½ million that decasualisation would save the Unemployment Fund. However logical, it did not appeal to the Treasury and there was some delay before they assented in a very half-hearted way to a course for which there was no precedent.

With the benefit of hindsight it is easy to say that both sides exaggerated the practical difficulties. How much would the scheme cost the port industry? What was the weekly minimum pay to be? For how many days a week should a docker be regarded as entitled to pay? Other practical problems obtruded from the smaller ports. How much would a man benefit who worked for six months with the fishing fleet? To make him a permanent docker would immobilise him during the fishing season, to his own financial detriment. By manipulating the many minor occupations available in ports such as Yarmouth and King's Lynn, the dockers there would certainly oppose being tied down to the one occupation of a docker.

The PLA took a major part in preparing for decasualisation. As their labour expert, I found it difficult to produce a workable scheme when none of the principals, as far as I could see, knew where we were going or what was required. This frustration was general, particularly among the less prominent and the less well informed employers. The simple questions to which there were no answers were: 'As an employer of dock labour how many men

are you prepared to accept as permanent on your pay book?'
Even by going back years and assessing the requirements from
work records it was not possible to say what future conditions
would require for a labour force. The number of dockers who
found employment in the port of London had fallen from 52,000
in 1920 to 34,000 in 1937. No employer was ready to commit
himself; no employer wanted to be short of labour as trade required. I produced graphs of attendance and columns of figures,
but none of these was conclusive enough to warrant the large sums
of money that decasualisation would require, if it was to be successful. It was with some relief that I heard on the six o'clock
BBC news on August 31st, 1939, that the Supplementary Reserve of the Regular Army was to be mobilised forthwith. I closed
my desk (it was destroyed in the blitz of 1941) on this and several
other problems that Hitler solved for us during the next six years.
The scheme was formally interred by an agreement signed on
October 30th, 1939, shelving decasualisation and paying the 14s.
per day demanded two years earlier. It was with genuine regret
that the more serious minded of the employers and the union
officials came to the conclusion that the climate of the phoney
war, and the drastic changes that developments would certainly
bring to the trade of the ports, was no longer favourable.

18

In the spring of 1938 the PLA had agreed to a War Office request
to help in the formation of No. 2 Docks Group of the Royal Engineers. No. 1 Docks Group had been formed as early as 1924.
Both were units of the Supplementary Reserve of the Regular
Army and were liable to be mobilised, as indeed they were, at the
same time as the Regular Army. My two fellow Investigators and
I were commissioned each in the rank of a Captain. The idea of
proceeding overseas immediately on a declaration of war that we
thought could not be long delayed was attractive. Getting in on
the ground floor of a new enterprise was to be preferred to subsequent impressment or a civil assignment somewhere in the
austere conditions of wartime England. We had time for two
annual camps before our organisation was put to the test. In our
1939 training we had many volunteers from the PLA staff, as
well as several labourers who had responded to the appeal for
stevedores. In the event, the three peacetime Investigators formed
part of the advance party that left Portsmouth for Cherbourg on
the day following the declaration of war. A week later, on the
arrival of the first convoy of warlike stores, we were greatly helped
by the sprinkling of dockers in khaki who had been recruited at
the dock gates a few days earlier and promptly put in khaki. They
were a skilled leaven for the 2,000 cavalry and artillery reservists
whom the War Office had thoughtfully provided to discharge
ships. Before the campaign in France had ended at Dunkirk, Stevedore Battalions, later amalgamated with the two Docks Groups,
had been formed and had been organised on a wartime basis. 'For
the first time in history the British Army has emerged from a major
war which has not produced a major transportation scandal.' So

wrote the Director of Transportation in his 1946 Report to the Army Council. In his next paragraph he gave his reasons for history failing so signally to repeat itself. The continued success of the Docks Groups (there were some dozen of these by 1945) were due, he said, to the unstinting support given by port authorities, the great railway companies and shipping firms, all of whom had encouraged their technical staff to enlist in one of the several branches of Transportation. Flattered as we were to hear of this appreciation, I knew very well that the consistent success of the military ports could not have been possible without the work of the dockers in uniform. History has always shown how unsatisfactory it had been to rely for working the supply ports on native labour or other auxiliary formations. Later in the war I had accretions to my command from several allied countries. I assessed their technical ability relative to the one hundred per cent accorded to my few British formations, made up mainly from enlisted port-workers. The response from London and other ports was, in fact, so enthusiastic that only the older men, and a few essential craftsmen, were left to cope with the subsequent inflow of ammunition and stores that reached these shores from the United States.

This is not the place to tell the story of the Docks Groups. To do so would be to shatter the anonymity that surrounded their wartime efforts. Occasional guesses in the Press to formations such as the Pioneer Corps or the Royal Navy were the nearest that war correspondents ever got to explaining the miracle that kept adequately supplied every army that the Allies put into the field. The London dockers helped to unpack the British Expeditionary Force in the first weeks of September 1939. Two weeks after Dunkirk in June 1940 they gathered together the scattered remnants of that force and loaded them, and such stores as they had, on ships for Southampton. None were left behind. The short-lived Second BEF was landed by them, re-embarked within a few hours and lived to fight another day. They had accompanied, two months earlier, the ill-conceived Norwegian Expeditionary Force and learnt how to discharge petrol and ammunition with enemy planes hovering above the port. They made life possible for the lonely garrison sent to Iceland at that time, as they made practicable the landing of British troops in Madagascar. They accompanied Wavell on his first dash across the Western Desert, opening the

Modern view of the West and South West India Docks. Two
of the row of eleven warehouses, built in 1805, that survived
the Second World War can be seen on the left of the picture.

Above   A grab load of bulk sugar being released.
Below   M.V. *Jean* discharging packaged timber at Newport, Mon.

Libyan ports while shells were still falling. In England, Transportation Groups were learning the technique of combined operations, how to discharge store ships three miles off a hostile coast, all knowledge which stood them in good stead in 1942 at the North Africa landings. In the summer of 1943 units of my command, No. 5 Docks Group, unloaded stores and ammunition off the beaches of Sicily and Salerno, and later, at Anzio, where the dockers in uniform dodged the 'jockey' bombs and worked their cargoes into craft whilst the parent vessels took evasive action.

On D-Day they came into their own. The War Office had built 'Mulberry', an artificial harbour, worked by Docks Groups who moved up later to the major port of Antwerp. They were content to get on with the job and to let the difficulties speak for themselves. In the Far East they worked under appalling conditions in the makeshift ports of Burma, proudly displaying their cap badge 'Ubique', for they were great travellers and were happier on the deck of a ship than on the barrack square. From Akuyrari, on the edge of the Arctic Circle, all the way to the ports on the West Coast of Africa, and on to Rangoon, London dockers froze or sweated in the holds of Liberty ships. They persuaded the worn-out winches to lift the last set of shells from coasters and Dutch schuyts, after they had been beached on the Normandy coastline. Their casualties throughout those six years were not light. From the explosion at Brest, in November 1939, on the petrol-filled *Pacific Coast*, and the ill-fated *Lancastria* sunk by enemy bombs as she was evacuating troops, including those from the resident Docks Groups at Nantes and St Nazaire, through the disastrous attempts to work cargo in the bombed port of Piraeus in 1941, dockers were a sitting target for enemy planes. Nearly every ship they discharged contained petrol or explosives, many of the latter being particularly volatile. That hardy trio Tobruk, Benghazi and Tripoli took a steady toll. My own headquarters port of Bari in Southern Italy was wrecked twice, once by an air raid and, as late as April 1945, by explosion. Each time some 1,000 casualties were suffered in the working area, of which Transportation troops bore their full share.

They learnt to take whatever Fate and the Brass Hats dealt them. During the landings off the south coast of Sicily one gang of about a dozen stevedores were struggling to complete the discharge of a vessel when the convoy commodore made the signal to sail. Despite their protests the ship's captain refused to take the risk of getting them back to the beach. He no doubt had a vision of how pleasant his wartime duties would be by the addition of a dozen hard-bitten and adaptable stevedores to his crew of very much diluted seamen. The coast of Sicily faded into the evening horizon and with it the square bashing and the whole of the military machine. Before these fortunate few lay an infinitude of lazy days, sailing through tropical seas, 'luv'ly grub' instead of bully beef and biscuits and the very occasional 'compo' rations. In due course they were struck off our strength. Their strange odyssey lasted for more than a year before their adopted ship put into a home port and Whitehall caught up with them.

It would be timely to wind up this brief account of the docker in uniform by quoting the only known breach of anonymity in which for six years he worked. The Prime Minister, in the categorical imperative for which he was known, signalled, during the particularly difficult discharge of stores and ammunition of the Anzio beach-head:

'Pray congratulate all at work at Bridgehead on record figures discharged on Anzio March 10, 1944.'

In 1948, on reading a book[1] on trooping during the war I came across the following: 'Those three weeks spent between the Clyde and Sicily in the midsummer of 1943 will ever be memorable to me. Many of our passengers . . . had worked in the docks of Le Havre, Brest and Nantes, during the B.E.F. days of 1939–40 *and were stevedores of the highest attainment, great-hearted giants, who cleared our holds when we did anchor off Augusta as I'd never seen them emptied.* Their quiet, happy and very efficient C.O. is in peace-time a PLA official as well as an officer in the Supplementary Reserve. He was carrying out his specialist work as a soldier from the very first day of the war.' I discovered later that the book was written by our OC shop, the a.m.c. *Letitia* of the Donaldson Line (13,595 tons).

Their last effort was one out of which only the troops engaged emerged with any credit. In 1948 the War Office re-formed certain units of the Supplementary Reserve. Among these was 81 Port Regiment RE which I had had the honour to form and to

[1] *Troopship* by Lt.-Col. R. A. Chell, D.S.O., O.B.E., M.C. Gale & Polden.

command. It was no fault of squadrons of this unit who landed stores and ammunition at Suez in 1956 that the campaign was a victim to hot heads and cold feet.

Meanwhile to return to the capture of the French coast by Hitler in June 1940; the wholesale bombing of London made it urgent to transfer ship discharge and loading, both military and civil, to the Clyde Anchorages and the north-western ports. Local labour was insufficient in both areas. Dockers and stevedores were brought from London, billeted locally and recompensed for the discomfort that the removal from their homes had caused. The military ports of Faslane and Cairnryan came into action by 1942. Together, the dockers both military and civil adapted themselves to these new conditions, and the country weathered the critical years; in 1944 the spotlight of war was shifted to the cross-Channel invasion.

When the force of the blitz abated the dockers returned to London. The Royal Docks and Tilbury had not been seriously damaged and from these two controls the major effort of loading and despatching store ships for D-Day was made. The new conditions imposed by strange types of cargo were met, and the urgency of the operation recognised, by the West Front Agreement. It was intended, and in this it succeeded, to ensure that tanks, armoured cars, ammunition and all dangerous, 'noxious, noisome and pestilential' cargo required to be thrown at the enemy, was discharged through the new Mulberry Harbour. To do this it had to be loaded to a schedule in London whatever the conditions there might be. In the event the operation proceeded without serious interference, The piecework rates agreed were more than generous; by those dockers who were not taking part in the operation it was stigmatised as 'Patriotism by the Pound'. The disturbing effects of so much easy money lasted well beyond the conditions that had led to the agreement.

19

Although the climate for decasualisation had been adjudged unfavourable in the autumn of 1939 and the collection of graphs, statistical tables and conflicting suggestions had been dispersed, the appointment of Ernest Bevin as Minister of Labour in the Coalition Government of 1940 quickly put the problem into the industrial foreground. The sudden changes in his working conditions had left the docker almost completely outside the many national agreements that guided his peacetime working. The wartime scheme implementing the principle of 'work or maintenance' operated from 1941. The Dock Workers (Regulation of Employment Act 1946 put it on to a peacetime basis. In 1947 the scheme was strengthened by the removal of certain anomalies and the controlling board was henceforth known as the National Dock Labour Board. As 'The Board' it has been known for more than two decades; even with complete decasualisation it operates in a truncated form for amenity and social functions. At its inception Bevin knew that it would take a generation before peace and general satisfaction were brought to dockland by the Board. During the many industrial troubles, stoppages and disputes that have marred the industry since 1946 the Board has stood on the side-lines, content to record the number of registered men at work, save when a particular dispute has been aimed directly at measures taken by the Board.

Its constitution and daily methods of working are simple. The original Board consisted of ten members, representing the employers and the union, with an independent chairman. There is a general manager for the day-by-day work of the Board. Local boards, constituted on joint lines, are responsible for the work of the national Board in each port. It is essential to bear in mind that *the NDLB exists for the regulation of dock labour. It acts as an agency supplying labour to the employer. The Board has never employed labour.* It has entered the docks as a third party. It keeps a register of men who may be employed on transport work.[1] It also keeps a register of employers who may employ the registered dockers. It maintains an interest in the growing number of permanent labourers employed by the larger employers. Registered men, other than these, were in the 'Pool' of labour and hence were known as pool men. They were allocated at each of the twice-daily calls in accordance with the demands of the employers. Also they were paid weekly by the Board, on returns made by the different employers for whom they had worked during the week—with money, of course, provided by the same employers. When no work was available pool men became entitled to 'stand-off' payments, less than what they would have earned at work, for each period of idleness. This did not prevent their taking work of a local and casual nature in other industries. The money for these 'fall-back' payments came from a levy paid by the employers on the amount of their wage bill. It was a percentage payment and was adjusted at six-monthly intervals in accordance with overall trade conditions. This is an incomplete account of the scheme which now exists only in the truncated form already referred to. It makes no mention of the excellent welfare and medical work done by the Board out of money provided by the employers. It is sufficient to show that the casual labourer, once he obtains registration, could live and keep fit during periods of unemployment. The conditions of his drawing the fall-back, familiarly known as 'bomping-on' from the sound of the rubber stamp impressed on a man's card, did not exclude his seeking and getting seasonal work, particularly when port work was slack. Thus work or maintenance replaced the inhuman conditions that had been accepted for over a hundred years.

Attention must however be called to the major weakness of the scheme. It was inevitable that it should treat men as units of

[1] Defined in the 1946 Act as 'employed or to be employed in or in the vicinity of any port or work in connection with the loading/unloading movement or storage of cargoes in the preparation of ships . . . for the receipt or discharge of cargoes.'

labour. Throughout the history of dock labour there has run a luminous thread of personal regard as between employer and employed. Not that the representatives of the National Association of Port Employers in conference round their mahogany table in Leadenhall Street knew the technical efficiency, far less the domestic background of any of the men they employed. This knowledge was reserved for the lower strata of dock managers whose efficient handling of the daily work was based on their personal knowledge and regard for the men they habitually employed. I speak here with some feeling because as a young officer, I felt responsibility for the permanent men and the 'B' men on my department. This feeling, which was shared by my brother officers and by officers of our grade working for private stevedores, was completely at variance with the statement officially publicised that 'there was not and had never been any personal relation between the employer and the dock labour'.

A time-honoured practice of master stevedores produced the 'choice' gangs. These were made up of men who satisfied their immediate employer and who, for his part, did his utmost to retain them. Under the scheme five excellent gangs that finished a ship at noon should be returned to the pool, there to be broken up into parts for other employers or else stood off. This was despite the fact that their employer had work for them on another ship arriving on the night tide. Small wonder that out of his own pocket he kept the five gangs 'out of the way' for the afternoon. This and other practices were accepted by both sides. As practical men the local committees knew that what was a fair deal on paper did not always commend itself to the men who had to get the work done.

Dock labour did not find it easy to accept the powers of discipline that the Board had been given. Although these operated against the employer, their impact was felt mainly by the docker. A pool man, fined or imprisoned for an action, such as pilferage, that reflected on his standing as a dockworker, or was defiant of the Board, could and did have his registration suspended or withdrawn and thus his work in the docks came to an end. I remember once, in the 1920s, enquiring after the health of a permanent man whom I had not seen for a week. With a sideways glance the ganger said: 'He's been sent up for a week.' I didn't enquire what he had done; it was no business of mine, and his job was not prejudiced.

There were rights of appeal; I was a member for five years of the London Appeals Tribunal and I can say that it was as fair and impartial a body as a Service Court Martial. Capable as the Board were in disciplining individual workers they found themselves completely outpointed by mass defiance. In 1949 the their chairman attempted to assert his authority[1] after a state of emergency had been proclaimed. His action was immediately repudiated by the then Prime Minister and he himself was summarily dismissed, *'pour encourager les autres'*. This did nothing to improve relations between the Board and the dockers.

In the immediate post-war years, successful efforts were made by NAPE to increase the permanent dockers among certain of their members. Not unexpectedly, bearing in mind the ingenuity of the docker at finding reasons why his lot should not be improved, the Blue Union opposed these moves. They 'worsened the position of the remaining casual workers' and they, it was asserted, took away the freedom of the individual to work when and where he pleases. It was our old friend 'three days on the hook, three days on the book'. Whilst for over a century the docker had campaigned for the right to work, he now asserted his right not to. In 1948 the PLA decided to increase their force of permanent labourers, which had fallen to 1,649, to some 3,000, only to find that there was no rush. The trickle of applicants took over a year before numbers reached the level authorised.

In 1946, after a short period as Assistant Superintendent at the West India Docks which was marked by the welcome resumption of the Jamaica banana traffic, I was appointed to the office of Traffic Superintendent. The duties were not well defined; the Board remit mentioned the need for co-ordinating the duties of the five Dock Superintendents. In practice it meant that all the sticky jobs, labour particularly, that could not be solved locally, found their way to my desk. At the same time I was expected to act as a buffer between the docks and my immediate chief, the Chief Docks Manager, responsible directly to the General Manager. The five years I spent trying to do this were the most valuable

[1] The strike, over a dispute on bulk grain discharge, was known as the Canadian Ships' Strike.

in my career. With a wry satisfaction I kept a daily graph of disputes, stoppages and strikes, few of which reached the Press. Conditions were sufficiently bad to justify my contention that, as each stoppage came along, we were back to normal. The days when the labourers throughout the port were happy in their work were abnormal. One of the many Commissions of Inquiry with which employers were pestered in the decade after the war considered the circumstances of the major, and also thirty minor, strikes. A disquieting feature of the period was the increasing repudiation of agreements by labour. The absurd position arose of a Blue Union leader repudiating an agreement that he had himself been instrumental in negotiating. The word of a union leader became of less worth than the paper on which it was written. This was largely caused by the rise of the unofficial leader.

All these unhappy occurrences were acted out against the background of a blitzed port, an unprecedented flood of exports, the urgent need to turn scarce shipping round quickly, and a shortage of materials, labour, and staff, with which to reconstruct and repair damaged berths. A minor but incessant irritant was the responsibility accepted by the PLA, following a wartime order, to provide meals and tea for all dockworkers. Despite the miracles almost daily performed by a dedicated staff, and the equipment sadly in need of repairs that were impossible to get done, no allowances were made by labour. Nearly every day, somewhere in the port, a local stoppage would have to be settled, because the mobile canteen was ten minutes late at a particular berth or the tea was not to the taste of a gang. Breakages and theft of tea mugs reached a figure of 800 a week and jeopardised the entire catering service. After putting up with these incessant and unreasonable complaints for five years it was with some pleasure that later, at the Surrey Commercial Docks, I had to consider the closing of an uneconomic canteen. It was midday, and, as I stood talking to the Catering Officer, a docker watched by a gang of his fellow workers came out of the canteen. He carried a plate of fish and chips. Thrusting it under my nose he demanded : 'What do you call this?' I looked at his uncouth face and said : 'I don't call it anything. If you don't like it, you can go outside for your dinner. And you can tell your mates I'm shutting down this canteen at the end of the week.'

20

This narrative has now reached the time in the history of dock labour when an entirely new factor shattered conventional port working. How this silent revolution came about, and no one concerned in its introduction in 1946 could possibly have seen where it would lead, and also the permanent effects it will have on the present and the future employment of dockworkers, I shall now tell. It can be summed up in one word: 'Mechanisation'. From 1946 until 1951 I was Chairman of the Mechanical Equipment Committee appointed by the PLA and charged with the introduction of machines into dock working. For a further five years, until 1956, I had the opportunity as a Dock Superintendent to put precepts into practice. On my retirement, the Surrey Commercial Docks was the most highly mechanised control in the port of London. I put forward the first-hand knowledge gained in these ten years as justifying the conclusions I have drawn. From 1957 onwards they have been confirmed by what I have seen of mechanisation in European and other ports, first as Technical Secretary to the International Cargo Handling Co-ordination Association and later as a Port Operation Adviser to the United Nations Technical Aid Bureau.

Mechanisation, which began as a series of independent experiments, has developed into a recognised technology. The selection and the purchase of the machines, expensive and scarce in 1946, had to be co-ordinated and not left to individual preference or the blandishment of salesmen. When they were put to work, it was found that certain laws operated. In the application of these laws, unheard-of results in cargo handling were obtained and scope for greater developments was revealed. Because the trend towards machines to replace manual labour was world-wide no port could afford to neglect the new methods. Not only was the nature of the cargo unit radically altered but the design and construction of ships, berths and port installations, clamoured for change. As Traffic Superintendent and Chairman of the Mechanical Equipment Committee I came into this most exciting phase of dock work from the beginning. I took an active part in the building of the new kind of port that mechanical handling demanded and which was to supplant that in which I, and six generations of my predecessors, had been reared. Whilst I was knowledgeable on the mechanics of the new methods, I confess to having my eyes closed to the profound changes in the world of dock labour that were a part of these. No one man can be censured for not being beyond his own age, and my colleagues and I can plead, with port operators everywhere, to being so occupied with the physical changes for which we were daily responsible that we could not see two decades ahead.

Using machines in place of hand labour called first for a backward look. Of what does cargo handling consist? Surely the picking up and the putting down again of innumerable units of cargo. From the time when the bag of cargo is taken from its stowage in the hold and, with others, made into a set, until the time when it is put on to a lorry at the rear of the shed, having in the meantime been taken by a hand truck from the ship's side, transported into the shed, put on to a pile, broken down again and trucked to the delivery bank, it is picked up and put down five times. Cargo that has to be sorted, graded or measured will get even more handling. To make this process possible, accepted as it has been, for a hundred years and more, the cargo unit had to be of a size and weight that could be manhandled, not only in the dock stage, but during its whole journey from, say, a packing station in Mauritius to a sugar refinery in London or Liverpool. Whilst it was possible to handle heavier packages by ships' winches or quay cranes, this advancement in cargo handling could not be implemented whilst other links in the chain of transportation consisted of pack-horse transport or native porters. No great advance in technical thinking was needed to see, in the reduction of the number of cargo units, a quicker turnround of ships in port. The process was not a quick one; for the need had to be demonstrated, both 'up country' and in the handling area beyond the receiving docks. It was very much helped by the work done by the International Cargo Handling Co-ordination Association (formed in 1951) and also the active co-operation of the International Standards Organisation. Through the work of these bodies it became possible to secure international agreement on the design of ships, dock sheds and many kindred matters. Contrary to the age-old traditions of security in all branches of technical discovery, there was a great outpouring of knowledge gained and experiments conducted in what rapidly became the new science of cargo handling. The need for the quick turnround of ships was paramount. In the inter-war years passenger traffic was generally accepted as keeping the liner companies going. Cargo handling, if it was given a thought in the City boardrooms, was regarded as the province of the Inward Freight Manager, a not very important person—or else the foremen at the docks. The loss of passengers to aeroplanes made itself felt very quickly after 1945. Liner companies were forced to examine the economics that had now to show a profit from carrying cargo, hitherto loaded so as to give the passengers a comfortable ride in a well-filled and stable ship, as the position had been explained to me in the 1930s.

The PLA were fortunate in having several senior officers who had served in Transportation units in theatres of war where the US Army had used forklift trucks and mobile cranes in their characteristically lavish manner. At Tilbury Docks a few of these valuable units had, in 1946, been left behind. The major incentive to mechanisation lay in the blitzed conditions on many of our quays. Even the most unprogressive of port operators could not put the clock back. With all the hand trucks in the port, sugar, wool and other commodities could not be trundled over the rubble that had replaced the well-paved quays of 1939. Our first attempt consisted of the landing and housing of bags of sugar. With a mobile crane we landed sets of sugar from a barge, dumped three sets at a time on a trailer and hauled this by a tractor across the uneven surface, to the warehouse. Here each set, still with the sling round it—we invented wire 'hairpins' to prevent the rope slings from slipping—was picked up by the wall crane, passed over the scale and hoisted into the upper floors of the warehouse ready for piling. With two men in the barge, the driver of the mobile crane, a tractor driver, and an attendant labourer we delivered the sugar to the warehouse with a gang of five men. When each bag had been transported by individual handtruck, the gang ran into double figures, with additional men as the distance from the barge increased. Faced with the manifest impossibility of restoring 1939 methods of handling, the union took a realistic view. Some genius thought of the term 'balanced gang' and this was found to be sufficient to cover the new approach. Instead of negotiating from the conventional gang and cutting out men not now wanted, we started afresh and built up the gang that would do the job. The fact that the number might be a third of the normal gang was not stressed. We were glad to get the work. It would not have been realistic to have approached the immediate post-war conditions in any other way. A prominent London wharfinger brought on an immediate strike by introducing forklift trucks, and a greatly reduced gang, with no warning. This became known as the 'DCM method'—don't come Monday—and it didn't work. There were three allies on whom we could count : the forklift truck, the mobile crane and the tractor and trailer. Before we could be sure we were using these the right way we made an analysis of dock work; there were machines for lifting and lowering cargo, for transporting cargo and for piling and unpiling cargo. I am sure that this was the first time that an analytical look had been taken at the day-to-day work. Not only were large sums of money involved in buying the new machines but we had to be satisfied that they could do the job better than it had been done manually, and that sufficient savings would be made to pay for replacement and for maintenance. Two discoveries of major importance were made almost at once. Firstly, it became possible in a great many instances *to take the machine to the job*. Hitherto the job had had to be taken to the machine. Logs of hardwood had to be taken by ship or barge to the Wood Wharves where sheds equipped with overhead gantries could handle them. Apart from the heavy daily maintenance, done in overtime hours, there was the tie-up of machinery capital that was not employed gainfully for more than thirty per cent of its lifetime. Mobile cranes would do the job equally well when not in use for general cargo. At the Surrey Commercial Docks we had produced for our timber piling a crane that would plumb to the back stowages in the sheds. During the off season, for six months, the jib extension that made this possible was removed and the crane was diverted to general cargo work. Being completely mobile, cranes could, at the cost of a couple of hours' overtime, be transported to another department or dock. Most dock cranes, particularly the expensive quay type, are grievously underused. Taking the machine to the job meant that we could use mobile cranes for an average of 300 days a year.

Our second discovery reversed the thinking of many generations. Dock transit sheds had settled down to a standard design with dimensions of about 500 ft. by 120 ft. and a low roof. The intention was always to get as much room under cover as possible. As additional money had to be paid for trucking cargo more than eighty yards from, or to, the ship's side, there was no point in making the shed too wide. Of jobs that required much sorting or grading it was said : 'You'll want Hyde Park for that.' Piling of cargo was resorted to during times of congestion only. The process was expensive, employed much labour and brought in no revenue. Piling was regarded as waste of money to be done only when necessary to keep the cargo flowing. Suddenly, overnight, the dock officer found that he could, with his forklift truck and his pallet loads, *pile cargo to a height of twenty feet, at no extra cost.* He could also transport pallets of cargo without any regard for distance. *Congestion and extra distance payments vanished overnight and so did the need for labour to earn them.* These twin bugbears of all conscientious officers disappeared with the use of the forklift truck. The transit shed, in its conventional form, was not, however, built for high piling. It was soon realised that new buildings, for which blitzed areas provided excellent sites, would have to meet modern piling conditions. Ground floors would have to be twenty feet high, railway banks would have to go. Internal buildings, such as offices, tackle sheds, lavatories and the like clutter, would need to be put outside. A shed that would hold 2,000 tons of cargo pitched up to ports could now take 7,000 tons piled high on pallets.

With these solutions in mind the problems of export cargo were next tackled. Conventional practice laid down that gangs of six men would receive cargo from lorries or rail wagons at the rear of the shed and each package would be trucked into the stowage earmarked for the destination port. The piecework schedule was based on an output of fifty tons in an eight-hour day. During the loading of a large cargo ship lorries piled up at the rear of the shed; it was accepted practice for work on 'striking' exports to go on each night until 7 p.m.

By using a mobile crane and a driver, one man to load the pallet and a forklift truck and driver to take away and pile these pallets in the shed, an output of some 300 tons a day soon became normal. By late afternoon the last lorry had been emptied and work was over by 5 p.m. Only a tithe of the former labour required had now to be employed. The annoying detention of lorries, with the dishonest practices that this had encouraged, also disappeared.

Progress was also made on the mechanical handling of green fruit at West India Docks and much labour was saved in what had always been a job prolific with men and handtrucks. At the Surrey Commercial Docks one of our most difficult problems was solved. Since 1820 when the first shipments of cut softwood, boards and deals, arrived in London, the handling of similar cargo had been done entirely by dealporters. They formed a closed shop in which some 1,500 men had found employment in 1939. By May 1951 this had fallen to 500. The work was arduous and did not attract the younger men and those home from the war. On being appointed Superintendent of the Surrey Commercial Docks I was charged with the mechanisation of softwood handling. I think the General Manager had his tongue well in his cheek, because the dock was admittedly the home of privilege and customs that had been undisturbed for years. My chance came very quickly. We decided to pile a parcel of heavy deals at the far end of a timber shed. As dealporters were liable, on their piecework rates to carry timber for a distance, if required, of one hundred yards, we were correct in demanding that the piling of this parcel be done. At the end of the first day's work I had a visit from the ganger who was also the union representative. He began in the customary manner : 'The lads have been talking about our job, sir,' and went on to explain how arduous it was. Their shoulders were sore and many had blistered feet. They had noticed that I was using a tractor and trailer to move gear and stores round the dock. 'One of the lads says he can drive a tractor.' In short, could they have the use of a tractor and trailer at 8 a.m. the next morning. I replied that all they had told me was provided for in the rates; tractors and trailers were for transferring gear and other domestic uses. It had never been considered that they could be used for cargo. I should have to consider very carefully the implications on the piecework rates of so revolutionary a change. In the end I agreed, with a proper show of reluctance, but with inward jubilation. Work previously done by a gang of fifteen or more men now needed only eight. The dealporters took to the tractor method like ducks to water and we soon bought a further supply of these useful pieces of gear. We were also able to employ them to bring back into use sheds that were a long way from the nearest landing point; once more we killed the bogey of distance. Next, we introduced the mobile crane for carrying and piling softwood. This did away with the cumbersome 'ways' up which the dealporters carried their loads or 'turns' to reach the upper tiers of their pile. To place, remove when finished with and to store these heavy deals, had taken a lot of ungainfully employed labour. It was fortunate that we were now able to get the work done with fewer labourers because imports greatly increased from 1951, while dealportering became decreasingly popular. When I left the dock in 1956 a 'hand' gang was becoming a museum piece.

Certain ships that used the dock brought very mixed cargoes from the Baltic. They had struggled for years to deliver their small parcels of plywood, wood goods and hardwood overside into craft. Discharge was slow, most of the working time being spent in dragging out partly laden craft and replacing these for new parcels which had shown up in stowage. I made an offer to the shipping company to mechanise this traffic. Landing the entire cargo on pallets, we took these away from the ship's side by forklift truck. In the quay shed we had, prior to the ship's arrival, bedded out the ground according to the cargo to be received. It was a simple matter to place each pallet load to its correct stowage in the shed. Delivery was made subsequently by road or by craft in the adjacent dock. After we had gained some experience of this mechanised handling the shipping company told me that, due to the quicker turnround, two ships were now doing the work previously done by three. They were now certain that time lost in the Baltic could be made up in London. After years of grumbling and complaints this was welcome news. The shipping line put up the money to rebuild a blitzed berth in the same dock so that ships of a sister line could enjoy the benefits of mechanisation. We also secured the quay work for the PLA labour.

Among our minor improvements was a revision of hardwood piling methods. These had been fixed in 1901 by agreement between the London and India Docks Company and the Hardwood Section of the Timber Trades Federation of Great Britain; they were based on the amount of timber that could be carried by a single horse load. In my early days in the West India Docks this was the accepted method; the very occasional lorry was not allowed near the sheds as it was thought that it might quite likely burst into flames. To load a pair horse van, piece by piece, took three men about an hour. The officer in charge of the department admitted that he had not seen single horse vans apply for timber since the early 1930s. We devised a method of piling by mobile crane that was based on a unit of one load, or about a ton in weight. This enabled a pile twenty feet high to be put up in a few hours. Three times the quantity of timber could now be piled in our sheds; deliveries were made in intact units, two to the width of the lorry, by mobile crane and the job took only a few minutes.

Gradually under the stimulus of the Mechanical Equipment Committee the accepted methods of handling cargo were subjected to a new look. Would they permit of being mechanised? Under an enlightened management we made pilot experiments. They cost money, something that the PLA and their predecessors had never allowed officers to spend without the certainty of one hundred per cent profit. From these experiments we learnt much and we saved large sums from being wasted. Not all dock processes, we found, could be mechanised. There will always be room for a few men and a few handtrucks.

A consequence of the post-war export drive that had to be tackled was the swing away from rail to the already congested and often inadequate roads. The docks generally had been built during the great rail era of the last century and none more so than Tilbury, which twenty-six miles from London Bridge, had relied entirely on rail connections with the City of London. There was in fact only one road in the dock, a primitive one on the north side which, it was rumoured, had been built, gradually, out of ashes obtained from coal-burning ships on the nearby berths. It had broken down badly under the stress of the tanks and armoured

No. 40 Berth, Tilbury Dock. Cellular Container ship of the
United States Lines Ltd being operated.

Left The author, 1969.
Below Dockers and other
trade unionists assembled
on Tower Hill for May
Day rally, 1969.

vehicles that used it duing the 'D-Day' embarkations at Tilbury Dock. It was urgent that it be replaced as part of a wholesale scheme for the reorganisation of road access to the dock that I was then considering.

The prime mover in its building had been Captain Andrews who, in the 1890s, saw the need for an approach road for the farm carts that brought eggs and vegetables to the crews of the many ships that filled the dock. He was an ex-mercantile marine captain who had devoted his retirement to bettering the conditions of the seamen of the period. We could find out little about him but we did discover, on some older maps of the area, that his road had been elevated to 'St Andrew's Road'. It was sufficient that we had uncovered the first case in history of the canonisation of a merchant marine captain. In the wholesale planning that converted the dock from a rail served to a road dock the effort of this Victorian worthy disappeared.

21

As with all revolutionary changes, the mechanisation of cargo handling was not the work of one man nor of one port. It was encouraging to us in London that Liverpool and Bristol were thinking along the same lines, not only in exploring the continued use of machines, but also in shed and warehouse construction. Later we were to learn that men's minds were working similarly in the ports of Western Europe. In some cases they had outstripped those of London.

The principle that underlay the new technique did not long remain a secret. It was too obvious to be locked away in the desks of the pioneers of mechanisation. Put briefly it ran : *'As all dock work is picking up and putting down again units of cargo, the larger you make the unit the less the number of operations required.* As the capacity of the new machines is not limited we can go right ahead and alter the accepted pattern of commercial packaging.' How did this work out ? Until London and Liverpool mastered the job of discharging sugar in bulk, early shipments were considered a nuisance. Originally imported in hogsheads since the time of George III, these were replaced by gunny bags as the jute industry developed. In the immediate pre-war years sugar in bags from Cuba and the West Indies, Australia and South Africa formed one of the staple commodities to enter British ports. The discharge of these cargoes, many carried in chartered ships, employed many hundreds of stevedores. Certain firms of master stevedores specialised in handling the heavy three-hundredweight bags of Cuban sugar. By a superb organisation, and a liberal labour allotment, outputs of 500 tons or more were achieved daily per gang. Almost as many dockers were employed in warehousing processing and delivering the sugar under the London Terminal Market conditions. It was a thriving industry; father and son had earned good wages on sugar but only the really fit could stand the pace. Suddenly, in 1949, the *Baron Haig* made history by arriving in London, carrying 5,073 tons of raw sugar in bulk. This was matched in the same year by 873,000 tons of sugar in bags discharged in London and 604,000 tons in Liverpool. By 1957 the initial difficulties, and they were considerable, of discharging sugar, a non-pulverulent solid, having been surmounted, 1,666,000 tons of sugar in bulk were imported and bag sugar had declined to less than 500,000 tons. Today, bag sugar is little more than a memory on which dockers in Old People's Homes dwell reminiscently. The unit, originally the hogshead, and then the bag, has become the shipload in bulk. Before long special ships were built that enabled discharge to be done more quickly than on the converted general cargo carriers.

Timber from Russia, the Baltic and British Columbia has, for a hundred years and more, employed probably as many men as sugar. In a recent year it was estimated that 272 million pieces of cut softwood were discharged in British ports. On the assumption that each piece was picked up and put down a dozen times, the number of handlings before a piece of timber came finally to rest as part of a building was astronomical. In 1958 I was invited to watch the discharge of a ship at the small port of Rochester. She was loaded with timber, made up into large packages, each a ton or more. Each package contained about a hundred pieces, the number depending on the thickness and width, but all of the same length. The timber had been sorted to size prior to shipment; each package contained pieces of one size only. Conventional practice had always been for the stevedores to dump timber, to the Bill of Lading, but containing many sizes within the one Bill, on the quay alongside the ship. In due course these huge dumps of timber (and in times of congestion one ship's cargo might have to be piled on top of an earlier arrival) would be attacked by a gang of dealporters. Picking up each piece they would measure it with the eye and then a 'turn' of half a dozen pieces would be placed on the shoulder of a 'strapper'. He would walk with his load to the place in the shed allocated to the piling of this particular cargo and then dump his 'turn' on to the pile. Two pilers would 'kick' the pieces into position and the pile was gradually built up. A gang with a long run from the quay to the piling position in the shed might need twenty men. The scrupulous sorting to size meant that each piece was handled several times. As I watched the packages of timber being discharged at the wharf in Rochester I noticed that each gang consisted of four men only, two on board putting a sling round the package, a mobile crane driver to land the unit and a forklift truck driver to receive it on the quay. The latter carried each package to a nearby shed and placed it immediately on to the final pile. Four men were doing the work that had for a century needed thirty or more for the combined gangs. Since 1958 the traffic in packaged timber, despite the many teething troubles that have been encountered, has now reached a tonnage that demands specially constructed berths at the new dock at Tilbury. Agreement has been reached on rational gang structures, that carries with it a completely flexible unit. Ships that would have taken a fortnight to discharge have been cleared in a couple of days.[1] At the time of writing (autumn of 1968) there is serious consideration being given to closing down the large area that has been the traditional home of softwood ships in London. The new methods of presenting cargo for shipment have, as with many others, had far-reaching results.

The oldest container in the history of our ports is the wine cask. Its origins are lost in the mists of history. From pre-Roman times, cask making and the shipment and handling of wine in this manner has been a major source of employment in ports such as London and Bordeaux. The twenty-six miles of vault stowage that underlies London Dock was built in 1805 in anticipation, soon realised, that it would provide work for dockers and profits for the company. Wine is now being increasingly imported in glass-lined containers. The installation for the reception and housing of wine in bulk, that will disappear with the closing down of London Dock, will be replaced by a similar facility at the West India Docks.

Frozen and chilled meat, landed in canvas nets and conveyed

[1] In 1951 a vessel with softwood took a master stevedore seven weeks to discharge at the Surrey Commercial Docks. She was a foreign ship with poor gear and was named *Semiramis*. The stevedores re-christened her, in recognition of her record stay in the dock, *Semi-eternal*.

to the delivery banks by electric trucks, has, for half a century, absorbed large numbers of dockers, including tally clerks and lightermen. A mechanised form of handling that takes care of the carcases from the ship's hold to the waiting lorry or rail wagon, has recently been introduced at the Royal Docks, making it possible to employ fewer men.

These few examples will give a clear picture of the way in which huge slices of the employment cake have, in the last two decades, been snatched from the hand of the docker. The lesser demand for labour has been evident from the consistent reduction in the National Dock Labour Board's Register. Had it not been for a corresponding rise in the tonnage of imports and exports and over-employment in the country generally, the falling demand for dock labour would have caused concern.

While industries importing sugar, timber, meat and wine are among those that have modernised their methods of presenting cargo for shipment, the many interests that are not identified with a staple commodity but which are responsible for exporting general cargo have also been active. Before the First War when biscuit makers in Dublin 'stuffed' their products in large red containers, each held about a ton of their products. Like the many other users of the London docks in those days I attached no importance to this type of cargo. Had anyone suggested that this was to be the pattern that the ultimate unit of general cargo would, in the next half-century, take, I should not have known what he was talking about. Like the forklift truck and the mobile crane, both invented and both half forgotten for decades, the container provided the scope sought by the pioneers of the larger cargo unit. Through the insulated meat container and the furniture van, the container has today developed into the shiny aluminium box that may measure forty feet in length and contain thirty tons of mixed merchandise. This is not the place to recount the difficulties encountered before the traffic in containers could pass the experimental stage. Led by farsighted American shipping experts the place of the container in modern commerce has now been accepted. There is not a sizeable port anywhere in the world that is not concerned with its chances of being included in the pattern of the forthcoming container traffic. Two consortia of British shipping lines are now (1968) committed to building container ships and to converting their present world traffic in break-bulk cargoes to carriage by containers. When it has been confidently asserted that the majority of cargoes shipped from Australia to this country could be shipped in containers, there is little room to doubt the serious approach that is now being made. The 'great savings' that the experts have in mind refer to the very small and specialised labour force required to handle containers. During the summer of 1967 I watched on one of the new berths, built at Tilbury Docks especially for the new container ships some of which were already working, an operation that left me speechless. During a long life spent in handling cargoes in many different ports and countries, I have never, in a matter of a few minutes, been so shaken by the potentialities of what I was then witnessing. From one of the new sheds emerged a thirty-ton capacity forklift truck, driven by a young docker. Sliding its forks under a full container it reversed into the shed and placed its load ready for shipment. This very ordinary young man, albeit a skilled truck driver, moved four containers in this manner during the five minutes that I stood there. I realised that I was watching something that none of my predecessors over the six generations during which men like me had worked in the docks had ever seen. One man had 'struck' about 100 tons of exports in a few minutes; shortly, the containers would be put on board with the same minimum labour and effort. Package by package this would have provided work for twelve men for twelve hours on the shed bank alone. A typical ship discharged 241 and loaded 107 containers in twelve hours, 4,200 tons deadweight of cargo. For 3,000 years the handling of cargo had not substantially altered; now, ships that took a week to discharge with 200 men were being turned round with a complement of thirteen men in a matter of one tide only. The full implications of this revolutionary change are only beginning to be realised. Interests, important because they have played so large a part in the handling of general cargo, such as the lighterage trade, British Rail, the road haulage combines, coastal shipping and the shipping and forwarding agents as well as the large body of tally clerks, will all find a sudden decline in the demands for their services. The cosy structure that includes all the above and many others gainfully employed in our ports had started to disintegrate. The process will be accelerated as containers get more of a hold on the general cargo-carrying

170

traffic. Official opinion was shocked by the McKinsey Report of 1967. The dispiriting assertion was made that by the mid 1970s, ninety per cent of the present labour force in the docks would not be needed. However much this was officially deprecated, it was accepted by those directly connected with the physical change-over from break bulk to containers. They wondered whether it would come earlier than predicted.

With the gradual passing of the general cargo ship go the uncertain factors that surrounded international shipping and many of the inherent disabilities from which it has always suffered. Delays to the arrival of ships caused by faulty arrangements for bringing forward cargo, unpredictable strikes and go-slows in foreign ports, lack of a complete knowledge of a vessel's contents and the order of stowage, delays in discharge through damage to cargo and the salvage element, all these deterrents to quick discharge will cease to have their present importance when they are replaced by container ships. Only weather will remain. The inflexible organisation required before a shipload of containers can be discharged, and another shipload put aboard simultaneously, can be likened to the apex of a pyramid, broad based in transport arrangements that cover the whole process from the producer to the consumer. The reception at the container berth of a full export load and the dispersal of the import load is, to me, far more impressive than the routine job of actual discharge or loading. It is now being helped by computers. Tied to their home port it is unlikely container ships can be switched to near Continental ports whenever there is labour trouble in the UK ports.

A few years ago I was taken round the port of Antwerp by a Belgian shipowner. I commented on the number of British vessels discharging on the quays there, before I remembered that, at the time, there was a strike in London. 'The British docker is the best friend we have in Antwerp,' I was told. 'At the Annual Dinner of the Antwerp Master Stevedores we always raise our glasses to him.' In the near future the industry will become more certain and predictable when some of the causes for the centuries-old alternation of boom and slump is removed.

I think that the present position, where (1969) general cargo still predominates as against that which will prevail within the next decade, can best be compared by looking at what happens now. Two ships A and B arrive on the same tide; it is Sunday afternoon; ship A has 9,000 tons of general cargo to discharge and this will take a week. Ship B enters with a small tonnage loaded at Rotterdam and will complete her full loading by the following Friday night when she is due to sail. As both ships arrive on Sunday they remain on their allocated berths until work commences on the Monday morning. Then all is bustle and movement, with made-up sets of small cargo units swinging overhead, barges being loaded or their freight taken aboard. Everywhere on the two berths there are labourers pushing handtrucks, driving electric trucks, or transporting pallets on forklift trucks. Tally clerks, lightermen, rail staff and road carmen abound; the voice of the foreman is heard in the shed and the many subsidiary firms that gain a living out of ship turnround are happily active about their several businesses. Both ships work merrily away, the weather is good, there is reasonable overtime to gladden the hearts of labour and staff and to increase their take-home pay to the figure that they had expected. Behind the general satisfaction, shared also by the port authority at seeing its berths fully occupied, and by the shipping companies who see their schedules maintained, there is the comfortable feeling that next week will see a repetition. It is true that no port authority with whom I have had dealings, whether in Europe or at the other side of the world, from Ireland to the Far East, has ever been fully satisfied with the way that their port is run. However, the day-by-day work does, when well done, provide a satisfaction that is often due to the knowledge that in dockwork the impossible is merely that which takes a little longer.

Look now on the other picture. It is, again, a Sunday afternoon, and a full container ship passes through the dock entrance and ties up at the container berth. Here she is met by a skeleton gang of thirteen men. Immediately the hatches are uncovered (of the single pull variety put in motion by pressing a button) the crane driver takes out the first container from its cell; he replaces this with an export container and this double operation continues round the clock, if the cargo lasts that long. As containers are landed they are taken away by road, rail, or perhaps craft, further exports being received by the same means. By the morning tide on Monday, it is unlikely that any cargo will remain in the ship for landing or that any cargo will be unshipped on the quay or in craft. Having made a cargo turnround the ship will be ready to sail. During the few hours that this work has gone on it will be comparable more to that of a well-run factory than to the dock to which we are all so well used. Consider the container crane that discharges and loads in alternate motions; reflect for a moment that this is the first piece of dock mechanisation (leaving out the piling machine and the grain suction plant) that does not have to spend half its working time getting ready for the next spell of effective work. When the normal quay crane has dumped its load on the quay, it cannot bring any more cargo ashore until its jib has returned empty to the ship's hold. Only with containers has it been possible to so 'homogenise' the cargo that a return load is both available and acceptable during each crane cycle. The docker trucking his bale of wool from the ship's side deposits it in the allocated stowage in the shed. He then has to push his truck back to the ship's side for another bale; the dealporter, who carries his turn of deals from the dump on the quay to the pile in the shed, has to walk back again. Even the electric truck has to return empty before it can pick up its next load. I remember, half in joke, when considering a claim from the dealporters for more money, twitting them on working for only half the day. Pressed for an explanation of this, to them, astonishing statement I reminded them that half their time was spent ungainfully walking back for their next load; they agreed that man, as a machine, was not a very perfect one, neither had the organisation on the dockside been sufficiently improved to make him one.

The container ship having sailed, after making a minimal demand on labour, staff, lightermen and others, the berth[1] will remain empty of ships for the rest of the week.

No supporter of the principle of quick turnround for cargo

[1] The United States Line terminal at Berth 40 at Tilbury Docks has a shed crew of thirteen PLA dockers working under a foreman. They have achieved a flexibility of working which enables the ship to be dealt with immediately on arrival, including week-ends and Sundays. The vital importance of the latter guarantee was the reason that the dock was chosen. The *American Lancer* on her first visit in June 1968 discharged and loaded 3/4,000 tons of containers, equivalent to six days' work on general cargo requiring over one hundred men. The target is to turn the ship round before the next tide after that of entry into the dock.

ships would be blind enough to assert that there is an unlimited supply of cargo waiting to be loaded on to ships whose voyage turnround has been cut by two-thirds of the time previously spent in port. Quicker turnround will not cause timber to grow more quickly nor the sugar cane to ripen earlier than the time that nature has appointed. In the long run, the arrival of general cargo at the loading ports which has now been phased to meet present sailing schedules, based on the present time spent in ports, will accommodate itself to the quicker turnround of container ships. Fewer ships will handle the same tonnage when it is packed in containers. These and other problems are serious and will not be solved overnight. What is perfectly clear and demonstrable is that only a tithe of the present dock labour will be needed to achieve the same amount of tonnage turnround. It is, in fact, estimated that by the early 1980s eighty per cent of the world's cargo will be carried in containers.

This and similar predictions, such as the one that I heard made in Hamburg in 1957 that the 'roll on, roll off' ship would put the conventional cargo carrier into the horse and buggy class of transport, should be accepted, however, with the reservation that much may happen during the next few decades. A great deal will follow if present negotiations for a more flexible approach by labour are successful.

At present there are in London alone some 1,500 tally clerks who record the number and condition of every unit of cargo discharged or loaded. It is difficult to see what place, if any, they will have on a container berth. Another casualty of the present system, and it was heralded as far back as 1948 with the first 'roll on, roll off' berth at Tilbury Docks, will be that sacred cow, piecework, which was designed, improved, and constantly revised so as to cater for all kinds of cargo. The port employer, and the docker, has now become largely the prisoner of the working conditions to which piecework has been made to fit. The 'continuity rule' which was intended during the Second War to give a fair share of the good and the bad jobs was made an excuse for some gangs refusing to commence work unless they were fully manned. In the immediate post-war years it was known for a ship with four discharging gangs, each one man short, to do no work for the first four hours of the day. The obvious course of 'milking' the gangs to make up three working units was not accepted by labour under the piecework arrangements. Detailed pay systems to cover every hour of overtime that could be worked throughout the year were agreed, further restricting the employer's freedom to take on or to pay off labour. The young and lusty stripling of container traffic could not be put into the straitjacket that had, for too long, confined the working of general cargo. Neither would the conditions of container traffic demand the all-out effort from the men that piecework had, as far back as 1890, been devised to extort. I remember once posing the problem to a union delegate whether all piecework was not a reproach on the honesty of dockers to give a good day's work for a good day's pay. I was young at the time or I should not have put so naive a question to an experienced docker. The pattern of the future will certainly be that of a small shed gang of specialists, working on a high daily rate of pay justified by the phenomenal output they will achieve.

22

On the first anniversary of decasualisation a report appeared in the technical Press that the 350 men employed on the South Quay at West India Docks had adopted a realistic outlook to changes they could already sense. To survive, a port today must not be a five-day working area with emergency overtime that only too often has become the 'old pals' prerogative, but a seven-day port where overtime is worked without question. At this dock, the South Quay has two modern berths built immediately after the Second War. The quay work was built up on the latest mechanised methods by my late colleague, E. A. Lewis, who shared our early struggles to introduce forklift trucks into the difficult conditions of fruit discharge. The new working arrangements provide for a rota of men for overtime working; each man knows when his turn will come. There is complete interchangeability between the ship and quay gangs. The area is now one big work-sharing community. 'Who does what' no longer matters, neither are the men here concerned with what is going on in other docks. The experiment, and the men are determined that it shall succeed, could be the pilot scheme for other working areas. It is completely in step with the trend in cargo handling and it proclaims an understanding by the dockers concerned of the imperative need to turn ships round. It cuts across the worst of the restrictive practices that have become 'customs of the port'. It is not surprising that traffic lost is now coming back to the dock. This is another step in the transformation of the dockworker from the muscular moron to the forward-thinking and specialist operator. In this connection, figures recently published (August 1968) show that in the first six months of decasualisation dockers' average earnings rose by more than £8 a week to £29 8s. The high earnings of the increasing number of specialist labourers must have made a real contribution to this uplift. Three months of decasualisation brought a reduction of 4,000 in the dock labour force in the U.K. ports, down to a total of 56,000. By the middle of 1970 the employers aim to reduce this by a further 16,000 men. Developments in cargo handling may, if their present rate of acceleration can be maintained, make even this seem too small a reduction.

Proof that employers are in earnest was given when seventy-four permanent labourers on August 30th, 1968, accepted severance payments. All these men are under 65; fourteen of them were given a 'bronze handshake' of £2,000 or more. They are the first of a batch of 833 men who have consented to the offer; half of them come from the London Docks. Pay-offs are planned to take place at weekly intervals, older and long-service men being given preference.

Many of the men who will receive, in dockland, such vast sums to leave the industry may be sons and grandsons of men who starved for five weeks in 1889 for the 'dockers' tanner'.

It is not necessary to stress that the reduction in the demand for the pivotal dockworkers is accompanied by a corresponding reduction in the need for lightermen and staff. Even were it likely that the tonnage of general cargo at present lightered in the port of London would be maintained in container form, the immensely quicker turnround of craft would knock the bottom out of the fleet of over 4,000 barges recently in the port of London. Changes in cargo handling had already caused a drop in the tonnage carried, from thirteen to nine million tons between 1963 and 1966. An estimate by the trade suggests a reduction from 3,000 to 1,000 barges in the near future.

A reproach to the industry has always been the paper jungle that has to be penetrated by the shipper or receiver of the smallest Bill of Lading. Valiant efforts, of which the Swedes were the protagonists, have, in the last decade, resulted in a standardised form of documentation. Container shipments can be carried out with the minimum number of documents; a minimum number of staff, aided by computers, will handle these.

While all these trends to simpler cargo handling have been operating, one inescapable conclusion has been forced on port authorities. Berths here and there in ports have become obsolescent. They have been replaced by a series of up-to-date installations. In the new dock at Tilbury there is a concentration of berths for container traffic, packaged timber and bulk grain. When in 1805 the London Docks were opened for ships, and this was followed in 1828 by its near neighbour, the St Katharine Docks, they met for a century and a half the needs of commerce, albeit the size of ships increased and this put the emphasis more on the warehousing side of their business. Now they have been closed; for shipping on September 30th, 1968, and for goods at the end of the year. Tilbury Docks, which from its opening in 1886 was the white elephant of the port, and saved only from a premature closing three years later by the revenue earned by the London Docks Company, has now become the hub of the modern port. In the process, the upper docks have outlived their times and their usefulness. In 1947 the Export Dock of the East India Dock was sold to the Poplar Borough Council for a new power station. Now, the Import Dock there has been disposed of. There is serious talk of selling the large area occupied by the eighty-odd berths reserved for timber ships in the Surrey Commercial Docks, the largest enclosed timber storage in the world. The future of the Regent's Canal Dock in the port of London owned by British Waterways Board and next in line with the London Docks is causing concern. Instead of the twenty-five ships that occupied berths ten years ago there are now two. No dock with so few attractions to modern commerce can keep in business. If container traffic takes the path predicted, the demand for general cargo ship tonnage must correspondingly fall. For some years there have been far too many ships competing for international trade. It was urged that continual new building was necessary because of the time ships spent in port. By 1950 the time spent by a cargo ship at sea had dropped to 130 days, from 210 days in 1929.

At this stage in the story it may well be asked whence came this sudden movement towards the larger cargo unit and the tragic (to the dockworker) results that have followed? Like many industrial changes, this came about through thinking on international lines, aided and encouraged by the International Cargo Handling Co-ordination Association and the United Nations Technical Aid Bureau. Many of those so engaged thought that no time should be lost in rearranging dock work so as to lead to the long-term elimination of the docker. They were taught so to think by the docker himself. No one has done more to encourage the container, the bulk cargo and the roll on, roll off ferry, and even the growing tonnage of air freight, than the docker. His record since 1946 has been a tragedy to those whose business has made them dependent on his efforts. It has been adversely commented on in every report, and they have been too numerous to detail here, made by government enquiries into conditions of dock labour. Unrest in the ports has been world-wide. There have been two main causes: pay and working conditions. I have tried to show how complex are the latter and what a rich field they provide for manipulation of disputes. On the one hand, there is the power given to the docker because of the urgent need of ship turn-round. On the other, hardly a day passes where conditions do not provide grounds for demands for extra payment. A typical case might concern the discharge of bulk grain from a cargo liner. The grapevine has told the gang of cornporters that the ship is stemmed for a drydock in Antwerp on the following day. Output is so manipulated—and the dockers are expert at this—that at 4.30 p.m. there are left about fifteen tons. The ship must leave the quay not later than 6 p.m. to catch the tide. A demand for £5 per man is made. The officer in charge, knowing that this demand to clear the cotchel of remaining cargo is sheer blackmail, puts the demand to the shipping company who will have to pay, with a strong recommendation that it be turned down. The company have no option to paying because failure to conform to the sailing schedule would cost several hundred pounds. If no decision is reached before 5 p.m. the men walk off the ship. If their extortionate demand is met, as it usually is, they will buckle to and finish the ship easily by 6 p.m. While shipowners are unanimous that this kind of demand ('or else') should be resisted there are always good reasons why the fight should not take place on their ship. Every shipowner is in favour of an away match. During the time I was Traffic Superintendent, my chief was absent on the day when a ship loaded with cotton seed, arrived. The cornporters demanded an absurd rate for discharge by suction machine. Under the pretence of considering this I offered the job to a master stevedore who was willing to do the job with baskets. At 8 a.m. the following days the cornporters, on arriving at the ship, found the master stevedore in command. Their delegate suggested that I had not played the game and that I ought to have been there—I should have learnt quite a lot about my parentage and other personal details. My chief was aghast at the action I had taken, particularly as I had not mentioned the matter to the General Manager. Appeasement, which was largely official policy in the postwar years, never appealed to me.

Bad time-keeping has been a feature of dock work since 1946. Late starts and early finishes, with exorbitant breaks for tea, have reduced the working day. In Liverpool the objectionable habit of 'spelling', where a gang is supplemented by two men who take it in turns during the day to withdraw their labour whilst remaining on pay, is barefaced robbery. Among the dock area in London, the main roads are cut by swinging bridges and these have to be moved to allow the passage of ships and craft. The swinging of each bridge has been controlled so that it does not impede men on the way to work, or those who have just left. Near the drydocks at the Royal Docks, the swinging of the road bridge was prohibited between 7 p.m. and 7.15 p.m. in order not to interfere with the drydock employees when they worked till 7 p.m. To meet traffic demands from ships and craft the bridge was swung continuously between 6.30 and 7 p.m. The men who were paid to work till 7 p.m. in the vicinity of this bridge, and who invariably ceased work at 6.30 p.m., were annoyed at being held up in this way. The union concerned wrote to me complaining of the injustice from which their members were suffering when they worked 'late'. I replied that I was sure that men who worked until seven o'clock at night had the undoubted right to proceed to their homes without catching a 'bridger'. We had gone to some trouble to make sure that the bridge was not swung between 7 and 7.15 p.m. when men working late could be expected to cross it; I had confirmed that this benevolent practice still operated. I had no reply, although I could imagine there were many verbal ones. This is mentioned as an example of the way of life that was only too prevalent at that period. The piecework system, and the national agreements, provided all the opportunities they could want to men who regarded the employers as simple people waiting to be plucked.

What was the union doing to allow all this blackmail to become respectable? The answer is, very little, and that too late. The Transport and General Workers' Union has many interests other than those in its dockers' section. It is a truism that men who work for their fellow men are badly paid and the union gets what it pays for, and very occasionally, a little more. The number of paid officers is too small for one always to be on the spot when trouble breaks out. When it is possible to locate an official, he is not probably the type to negotiate a satisfactory settlement. In the days of Ernest Bevin it was expected, and we were never disappointed, that an agreement we made locally would be honoured. Our word and that of the union official settled the matter. Of late years the latter has given up much of his powers as a negotiator; he is now little more than a messenger boy. Having agreed to the employers' case, having heard the local officer put his case, his only constructive response is to go back to the men to seek their opinion. The whole unhappy business will have to start all over again with the disgruntled and repudiated official showing less interest in the settlement. Although I was always on the other side, there were many times when my sympathies were with the union man, who had neither the power nor the will to discipline his members as Bevin would have done. This can be done only by a powerful man at the top. Since Bevin gave up his position as General Secretary in 1940, none of his successors have, in effect, said: 'What I say goes; if you don't like it, get out.' There are many people who wish well for labour who feel that the unions have needlessly handicapped themselves, and are still doing so, by not recruiting for their top posts from the world of management. If running a union and getting the best possible wages for the members is a serious business, as the latter believe it to be, then surely the one man responsible, the General Secretary, should come from the same world and be of the same management calibre as the employers with whom he has to deal. How can a man be a powerful figure, whose word is law, when he gets, and is known to get, the salary of a bank clerk? Whilst tyrannical and vindictive in many ways, labour professes to worship the sacred cow of democracy. The voice of 'the man in the body of the 'all' is still supposed to be decisive whoever planted him there. The 'statesmanlike' type, the high official who has a difficulty for every solution suggested, is too typical. Too much importance is attached to practical experience; its value lessens as the distance from the ship's hold increases.

With dock labour working in these unsatisfactory conditions, the emergence of the unofficial leader is inevitable. In any body of men together in a fairly confined space, conditions are ideal for the breeding of discontent and the engineering of industrial action. It may be that the cargo, on being uncovered, is seen, or is thought to be, in a damaged condition. The gang immediately see the possibility of forcing an allowance in excess of the piecework rate. Knowing that their 'just and reasonable demands', as they so picturesquely describe them, will be cut down, they pitch the amount at double what they will take. The shipping company, or the port authority's officer, having much experience, pooh-pooh the difficulties and offer a token allowance that would more than cover any delay in output caused by the condition of the cargo. The men know this, and if the gang is reasonable, they accept it and no more is heard of the dispute. There may be, however, one man in the gang who encourages the remainder to stand out and the dispute is then caught up in the conciliation machine. Eventually, an allowance, higher than the local figure, is obtained. The men say : 'If it wasn't for old so-and-so we shouldn't have got that.' He achieves some local reputation as a hard-headed negotiator : 'You can't pull the wool over his eyes.' He has won the first round and has put the employer on the defensive. He becomes known to the latter as a trouble maker and, whenever possible, in the days of the pool of labour, the local foreman will avoid employing him. This is enough to give him a small-sized halo as a martyr. *Tolpuddle is never far from Tilbury.* He will be careful to choose his own battlefield, and his own cause. As each round is won his reputation spreads. His services as a negotiator are sought by neighbouring departments. Although the union look askance at his activities as poaching on their own, the incontestable fact is that he does get results and they don't. He is on the spot when trouble starts.

The T & GWU have admittedly a very difficult task for the inherent nature of dock work provides a never-ending nightmare to the more conscientious officials—and many are dedicated men; they have to be. This cuts no ice with their members who regard their officials as paid servants. 'You should work for a capitalist, my boy, you'll only have one boss,' said the father of a colleague some years ago. 'I've been a union official all my life and every b—— who pays his 4d. a week thinks he can order me about.' He put his son into a private timber firm where he did well. The lot of the union official is not a happy one. Jack Dash, whatever people may think, is undoubtedly sincere in his concern over the lot of his fellow workers, particularly in the Royal Group of docks; the dockers there see in him an effective spearhead for the frustration they feel. The 1967 stoppage that lasted eight weeks ended in an impasse. There was no alternative to the union stepping in to patch up a peace, another 'derelict babe of strife . . . and mother of wars to be'.

Decasualisation introduced many new difficulties. Not even the most naive of employers conceived so revolutionary a change as taking place peacefully. Had all dockers been men of goodwill, which they are not, all might have been well. Firstly the allocation of the large pool of casually employed labour meant that every employer was saddled with a labour force that could not be gain-fully employed all the time. The bright boys would on occasion have to stand down; the less bright and the older men would have their turn at the good jobs. *Decasualisation in British ports did not, and could not, cure the casual nature of the industry.* It could not make ships run to schedule neither could it prevent stoppages in foreign ports. There still existed the position where one employer was short of labour whilst his neighbour had an excess. There had, with decasualisation, to be a high degree of mobility, men must be lent as required, whatever their personal feelings, and whatever effect this might have on the weekly pay packet. They must, if any personal feelings of loyalty to an employer is to result from de-casualisation, know that they will be returned to their own em-ployer as soon as the job finishes. And this brings us to the second snag, the Continuity Rule. During the Second War the loading and discharge of warlike stores presented a variety of jobs, some of which were distinctly unattractive; there was difficulty in get-ting the latter jobs manned. The slicker and the more active dockers 'found' the good jobs; the slower and the more lethargic, having been directed to the poor jobs, quickly deserted them. It was agreed, therefore, that the gang that commenced the hold must remain there until the hold was completely discharged or loaded.

An excellent rule on paper, it is only too obvious how unpleasant it could be to some and how rewarding to others. A wartime measure, it remained as a permanent irritant to dock working, mainly because, it was alleged, it protected the weaker members of the union. Argument is possible on both sides; it is sufficient to say that when manipulated by unscrupulous men, it can readily be exploited as a source of trouble. The third cause for strife is one that is as old as the hills. Prior to September 1967, dockers contained several distinct classes. Look at any Press picture of a dockside meeting. There are the young and active men, good truck or crane drivers, to whom any employer is pleased to give work. These men can so arrange their movements to ensure a pay packet that meets their domestic needs and yet gives them a day off whenever they choose to take it. They are better than their mates, and this fact is accepted. Next come the solid mass of middle-aged men who have achieved a standing with a particular employer. They are known and recognised as good workers and their pay packets reflect this. At the rear of the labour force are the old men, those nearing pensionable age. If not exactly passengers, these men expect to be carried by their younger and stronger mates, even as they themselves carried the older generation in their heyday.

The basis of industrial peace is a fair deal for all; the basis of our wartime rationing was fair shares for all. This did not prevent those who, strongly believing in the principle, had some useful contacts, from taking in half a dozen eggs or a pound of butter at the back door when opportunity offered. While I was a Dock Superintendent there was a period when labour was not sufficient to meet the daily demands. To ensure that all employers received a fair share of the labour available a daily meeting was called, when the several demands for gangs were pared down to the number that would be there the following morning. The scheme, which had been agreed by the shipowners, worked well for a week. It worked well until a prominent shipowner found that he was getting a fair deal. This left him with at least two gangs short each day of the number that he could have got under the free-for-all conditions. He explained personally to me as Chairman of the Labour Allocation Committee that a fair deal was a fine thing for the sick, lame and lazy. As his firm was none of these, he had been instructed from the City to withdraw from the scheme. That was the end of our little effort to do good. It taught me that no man of initiative and courage wants, or will tolerate, a fair deal. So it was with sufficient of the dockers when the threat of decasualisation became real. They saw the danger, and it was one that directly affected their pay packet—they would have to take work turns with newly allocated men. If there were insufficient work for all they would suffer a temporary loss of earnings. Such conditions can hardly be expected to commend themselves to the cream of the dock labour force who, by their ability, have been able to pick and choose their jobs. A fair deal which cuts their wages makes no appeal. Where everyone is equal under the national agreements that regulate dock work, surely some must be more equal than others, if justice is not only to be done but to be seen to be done. There is little doubt that as the younger and more adventurous dockers accept severance payments and leave the industry, and as premature pensioning reduces the older men, the situation will right itself. These difficulties, and there are others, have been described to show how hard is the path of those who would help the docker. As Mr Justice Devlin has said in one of his Reports on the dock industry : 'The docker dislikes change even when it is for his own good.'

23

After twelve months of decasualisation, the tangible results can be simply expressed, for the men, in greater security of wages and reduced hours of working; for the employers a faster turnround, and an opportunity to introduce further mechanisation and to agree to a new approach to the rigid conditions of piecework. Decasualisation cannot cure all the ills inherent in dock labour but it can, and it has, after only a short period, produced an atmosphere in which both sides can talk with reason and understanding. The two main unions have (1968) now agreed to local committees making improvements outside the structure of national claims—a big step forward.

Further encouraging signs are the passing of piecework as the dominant system of payment for cargo handling, the surrender of the 'who does what' principle, and the recognition by younger dockers that new conditions demand, and will get, a sensible response from a labour force that sees this as the only means of preserving their individual jobs and the trade of the port in which they work.

From what I have said about the trend in cargo handling it should not be necessary to paint a picture of the port of the future. It will still be a place that will fulfil the main purpose of a port, where cargo can be transferred from water-borne to land-served transport. The emphasis will now be on the nature of the cargo, unit loads, containers and bulk cargoes. No experienced port operator can see today's general cargo vanishing overnight, but they can glimpse the gradually accelerating process by which change will diminish the number of small cargo units and the dockers that will be needed to handle them. Although not with ports in his mind, Robert MacNamara, the late Defence Secretary of the United States, calls attention[1] to the education that an intelligent man would have received in third-century B.C. Athens, fourth-century A.D. Byzantium or fourteenth-century Bologna. In each case it would have been reasonable to have assumed that the education received as a child could still be meaningful in old age. The rate of change, if there was any, was slow enough, in relation to the life span, to make it certain that the education received in youth would still be valid in old age. Change, since 1946, relative to time, has been so merciless that those who stand on the side-lines, watching the disappearance of the world in which they have grown up, can agree certainly on one thing. Every year will see a lesser demand for dock labour until within a decade a few thousand skilled specialists in cargo handling will be found sufficient to move the world's tonnage through those ports which are necessary for the process. By then, decasualisation will not matter much. Continuity Rules and allocation of work, even piecework as a system for regulating dock employment, will belong to a dead past. While this will interest the social historian who sees the meaning of the tragedy that has overtaken the individual docker, it can have little importance for the relative few who will survive the cataclysm.

In conclusion, I can say that for many individual dockers I have had the greatest respect and liking. Both in the docks and in uniform one could have had no better men. In the port of Bari, in April 1945, the hulk of the *Charles Henderson*, on which 1,000 tons of bombs had gone up in flames a few minutes before, was boarded by half a dozen Sapper dockers. The remaining forward section, with a list, was on fire; 1,000 tons of bombs still remained in her holds. Cries were coming from Italian stevedores trapped in the main hold. All the civil workers were rescued. I think it was the bravest deed I have seen in two wars. The job was done in the same cool and unemotional way as these men would have landed a few sets of bag cargo. How can one not admire men of this calibre, typical of a class and a profession that breeds them by the hundred? It is impossible to look at the picture and to say that there are two classes—the workers and the employers. Unfortunately, there is a lack of stature on the part of those who are paid,

[1] *The Essence of Security*, Robert MacNamara, August 1968.

however poorly, to look after the dockers' interests. There is, on the other hand, a lack of contact between the employer and the man he pays. In my working life at the docks, I could count on the fingers of one hand the occasions when top management ever visited the docks to watch those activities over which they wrangled for so many hours in Leadenhall Street. The chances of 'the boss' ever being known or recognised by his men were remote. In a court case in 1868 between the Crown and the London Docks Company, in attempting to define the status of a certain dock foreman, the judge asked : 'Has he a name about the place?' When that desirable state is common as between the City and the docks then the docker will know that there is a management, above the foreman, to whom he can take his grievance and who will show some interest in him.

Mr T. O'Leary, o.b.e., the dockers national secretary, and a dedicated union official, for whom I have had, for thirty years, great liking and respect, and who has worked strenuously to bring about decasualisation, has put the position clearly. If the technical improvements going on now reach their logical conclusion, dockers will become technicians responsible for controlling the means of loading and discharging the ships of the future. He foresees a greater status for the docker—a status that decasualisation has already achieved and which will enable the men of the industry to go into public ownership on a higher level than before. There will be fewer dockers but they will have a larger share of the work. The docker should move into the stage of the established staff employee with all the conditions that go with it.

To conclude this account of the dockers' struggle and what it has achieved I would continue to quote Mr O'Leary : 'The day of hiring and firing dockers is gone.'

APPENDIX

		Some steps in the pay of dockers, 1802–1968		*Rate of pay* *per day*		
					s.	d.
1802	West India Docks	200 permanent				
		labourers appointed			3	6
1805	London Docks	100 preference men	Perms		4	0
		appointed	Casuals		3	6
1809	,, ,,	300 permanent men			3	0
1816	East India Dock	No mention of P. men			3	0
1828	St Katherine Dock	225 permanent men				
		200 preference men	Per hour			4
1839	London Docks	Additional 1s. 6d. weekly to the more				
		efficient preference men				
1850s	,, ,,					4
1872	West India Docks	Period of Prosperity				5
1889	All docks	Great Strike				6
1911	,,	Devonport Agreement				7
1920	,,	Shaw Award	Per day	16		0
1921	,,	Reduced to	,,	14		0
1922	,,	,, ,,	,,	12		0
1922	,,	Tied to cost of living	,,	11		0
1924	,,	,, ,, ,,	,,	12		0
1931	,,	Depression years	,,	11		2
1935	,,	Trade revival	,,	12		0
1937	,,	Decasualisation				
		demand	,,	13		0
1947	,,	After Second War	,,	19		0

From then on until Decasualisation on September 18th, 1967 hourly rates of pay rose steadily. Dockers' pay on that date was 6s. 6½d. an hour. Average weekly pay was £22 10s. 5d. without overtime or piecework earnings.

Since then further substantial demands have been made. The granting of these will be dependent on Productivity Agreements which can now be negotiated locally and independently of National Agreements.

INDEX